Soul Grasping Poetry and More

Phyllis Wiley

© Copyright 2006 Phyllis Wiley
All rights reserved. No part of this publication may be reproduced, stored in a retrieval system, or transmitted, in any form or by any means, electronic, mechanical, photocopying, recording, or otherwise, without the written prior permission of the author.

Note for Librarians: A cataloguing record for this book is available from Library and Archives Canada at www.collectionscanada.ca/amicus/index-e.html
ISBN 1-4120-9751-7

Printed in Victoria, BC, Canada. Printed on paper with minimum 30% recycled fibre.
Trafford's print shop runs on "green energy" from solar, wind and other environmentally-friendly power sources.

TRAFFORD
PUBLISHING

Offices in Canada, USA, Ireland and UK

Book sales for North America and international:
Trafford Publishing, 6E–2333 Government St.,
Victoria, BC V8T 4P4 CANADA
phone 250 383 6864 (toll-free 1 888 232 4444)
fax 250 383 6804; email to orders@trafford.com
Book sales in Europe:
Trafford Publishing (UK) Limited, 9 Park End Street, 2nd Floor
Oxford, UK OX1 1HH UNITED KINGDOM
phone +44 (0)1865 722 113 (local rate 0845 230 9601)
facsimile +44 (0)1865 722 868; info.uk@trafford.com
Order online at:
trafford.com/06-1507

10 9 8 7 6 5 4

Special Thanks

I want to give special thanks to the people in my life that has been a blessing to me!

My daughters Tonita Wiley and Tiwana Wiley for they have stood by me through the toughest of times. I want to thank them For taking the time to listen to me read my poetry even if they didn't feel like listening and supporting me in every way that they could.

Chelsea and Brittany my loving granddaughters for bringing me so much joy! My brothers who encourages me a lot and believing in me! For all of their support and encouragement, they always says I know that is a gift.

My father who is now deceased but in my heart he is the real poet, I remember him quoting many poems throughout my life, To my mother who has inspired me in more ways than one, she always prayed. Special thanks to Mr. Kwabena Asare of myfoto photographers and his lovely wife Justina Asare for her love and support. My God daughter Mrs. Tamiko McAlmon for her contribution and her love and support.

Last but not least I want to thank Dr. John Giusto, M.D and the many pastors who have allowed me to either share my poetry from the pulpit to the congregation or just simply listen to me read to them and encouraged me to get it published! Pastor Bennie Griffin, Gayle Holloway, Charles Pettiford, Theodore and Beverly Bryant, Michael Walrond just to name a few and the list goes on.

I thank God for everyone that has ever listen too or encouraged me in any way to pursue my dream of publishing my poetry.

May God bless you all

Soul Grasping Poetry

This is a book of poetry containing many of my life experiences as well as others. I feel a strong urge to write, I feel that writing is a mandate of a higher power it's something that chose me and not my choosing it. There are times when I cannot even sleep until I began to write poetry. I use to write letters to my brother's girlfriends when we were young teens. I have even felt such a surge that if I didn't write I would lose my mind. So I have written poetry for years only to tuck it away in the closet.

This book is compiled of poetry from pain and sorrow to joy and victory, I believe that there is healing through the poetry God has given me to write. I once shared a poem that I was mandated to write, and a young lady confirmed to me that she truly felt liberated from a pain she suffered for many years as a result of being raped by her own father. Many of the poems in this book are about real experiences that I have had in my life. Also there are stories that others have shared that are written as well, no need to sift through for whose who, I just hope one of them helps you or someone else. Then there is a little of personal birthday celebration of my loved ones and friends that is dear to my heart.

This is a book that all can relate to no matter the age, race, or gender. I am convinced that to every problem there is a solution. No one is a loser until they decide to quit. It is when you are hardest hit that you must not quit. Life is full of ups and downs, valleys and peaks, but

the strong must bear the infirmities of the weak... So this book of poetry is primarily about helping someone who may seem hopeless to gain hope and find strength in knowing that you are not alone in life struggles. We can celebrate life by helping to show someone else the way through love, forgiveness, patience, tolerance and endurance. Just simply share the truth of how you overcame adversity, share your testimony it just might bring another one hope, healing and liberty.

About The Author

This book is written by Phyllis Wiley who is a native North Carolina, the mother of two daughters and two lovely granddaughters. I feel compelled to share a fraction of my life experiences through poetry .I have overcome some real tragedies in life; I know as life goes on I am not exempt from test, trials and tribulations, I have come to terms that some times difficulties of life are just a part of the human experience. We all can share our experiences in an effort to help someone else make it through after we realize just how imperfect we all are. I believe that if you have overcome any difficulty in your life it is only to help someone else. We all travel down different roads in life but the end of life leads us to the same place, and that is an eternal resting place made possible by God through his son Jesus Christ.

I raised the two daughters alone with little or no help from the biological father's primarily me and father God. Speaking of fathers I watched my father begging for life when I was fourteen years old after being shot with a 410 gauge shotgun about four inches from his heart. He was not expected to live but his life was a true miracle, I was grateful to be a witness to the power of God during this tragedy in my father's life he lived many years afterwards. That experience really made me know that there is truly a God that lives. I am one of seven siblings and we all practically lived in the waiting room of the hospital for approximately one year or longer while my father was hospitalized during that miraculous period of his life.

I am well acquainted with grief, but full of compassion so I feel led to share some of my life experiences along with a few inspirational and personal poems I have written for others on both happy and sad occasions. I believe there is healing in the poetry that God has given me to write. I believe that someone will be able to cling on to hope and keep faith alive, so they can overcome the trials and pressures of life that we all have to deal with from time to time.

We sometimes suffer pain and loss and the devil wants to isolate us and make one feel as though they are the only one who ever experienced this kind of pain. But I am here to tell you that you are never alone. Don't ever give up on yourself and always forgive others as well as your self. Love and endurance will allow you to rise above it all, no matter what comes your way. Life is worth living, it only takes a moment for one's life to be changed, and one word can change your life forever.

Whatever you do don't ever stop loving people, especially yourself through the power of God you can even love your enemies. The truth of the matter is enemies help push you into your destiny. So don't stop loving. Finally I believe when one stop loving then we stop living life according to how God intended it to be. Without love it is impossible to please God and I am all about the agape love.

Please be advised that there are words capitalized in some sentences which may appear, incorrect but the Author chose this method to express emphasis on certain phrases

TABLE OF CONTENTS

Revelations 12:11 13
May I have this dance 15
My little angels 18
Real love can't die 19
Physical vs. Spiritually 21
To hate my sister is to hate myself 23
What about me 25
When you shot my mommy. 29
Who am I 31
What language do you speak 33
It's a new day 34
I do not know stability 35
Have you ever been to church 37
What will you do 39
I choose you 40
Class-room clowns 41
I can 42
Child abuse 44
Because you know not who you sit among . . . 46
And so she cries 48
Like the birds I sing 50
That's not who I am 51
And now I live 53
Cross burners 55

Fasting and Praying	57
Love isn't love	61
I know how to go on the down low	62
Unidentified heroes	63
Let my heart go	64
Single parents	65
The higher the eagle fly	67
Will a real christian stand up	69
When the pressures of life	71
How can one	73
Wise builder	75
When we teach hate	77
Wonderful workers of God	79
Whose knocking at your door	82
Where's my people at	84
Where my strength lies	86
When people care	88
When I was	89
Much too young	91
Today	93
In loving memory of my daddy	94
Respect	96
Something is wrong	98
Smiles	100
The death is in the wind	102
Pain free	104
Now what	106
No test no testimony	107

Nine eleven	109
My little bit of hope	111
Lonely but not alone, this time	113
Last night I saw a man	115
And God	116
But God	118
Let God	120
If God	122
When God	124
If eyes could talk	125
Life is yours to explore	126
Do what you like	129
A man is never a failure	130
Cause it's bothering me	132
Cause they using me	134
Feelings	136
Gods angel came upon me	139
Forgiven	141
I am	143
I am not here for me	145
I am still here	147
What's important to you	149
Who is your father	151
More than I want to see	153
My experience at the spa	155
Nice meeting you	158
Mr. Computer man	159
Mr. Spiritualily	161

I hear my brothers crying	162
Just Be Content	164
The Sun and the Sea	165
I Did My Part	166
You Ain't No Friend of Mine	167
I Feel You	169
I Am Grateful	171
Only One Star	172
Gang violence	174
Happy birthday Tiwana	177
Happy forty fifth birthday	178
Happy birthday sister	180
Happy birthday buster	182
Merry Christmas Angie	183
The golden candle	184
Eternal bread pudding	186
Farewell	188
Thank you	190
When the shack start burning	191
Uncolor me	193
The most dangerous stranger	195

REVELATIONS 12:11

And they overcame him (Devil) by the blood of the Lamb (Jesus) and the words of their testimony, and they Loved not their lives unto death.

This Poem was written, one day while I was sitting thinking about how, all of us from time to time will go through periods of loneliness in our life, and we sometimes feel all alone. I thought about how I had been let down so many times by folk I trusted and thought I needed.

I thought; how foolish I had been to think that another person could fix years of pain, fear, resentment, sadness, anger, bitterness, and confusion thrusted upon me in a place called home at a very young age.

It took me many years to begin to smile, and I mean that literally.
I invited people into my life who I thought would bring me Joy, but instead I got cut in open wounds. I have really been disappointed in people I trusted to be my friend many times: both male and females.

I found out only God can heal a broken heart and a wounded spirit, so while I was looking for void to be filled by others I only found more sorrow until I looked at the word of God and began to take it serious and Trust God at his word. I found out it was not really their fault that I experienced pain from the relationships it was actually mine; Why because Jesus says in his word that there is none like him. I went to everybody but him trying to fill a void. I believe that there is someone sitting under the sound of my voice right now that could possibly be in this same situation. LOOKING FOR LOVE IN ALL THE WRONG PLACES.

So we began to invite people into our lives sometimes that may not be the best thing for us. We will sometimes tolerate being treated without the respect or the kindness not only that we desire but that we deserve, So we suffer a lot of abuse, or pain all for the sake of trying to fill a void of loneliness or wanting to feel loved. It sometimes leaves us feeling angry, envious, bitterness, and sometimes just down right depressed.

Until we finally discover the Truth and realize the greatest Love really has to come from within. We have to Love ourselves enough to be happy with ourselves: With or Without someone else in our life. It does not necessarily have to be a spouse, I am talking about some of us just have to have a buddy or someone we call just to tell all our problems too. Not realizing they too have unresolved issues. I realize that only a God Kind of Love will help us reach a place of Joy and Peace within that cannot be destroyed. (That Agape Love) Understanding Gods Kind of Love allows us to really find true happiness and real Joy no matter what our circumstances may be.

Do you not know that there are people in mental institutions because somebody hurt them so bad, I'm talking about somebody they thought Loved them hurt them so bad that they could not get pass the hurt.

So this poem is about me and a few steps I took to truly be happy with myself, and to become my own best friend. I realized that if I refused to obey Gods Word, then I really was my own worst enemy. I was upset because I thought others didn't love me, but the real truth was I Didn't Love Me. I was neglecting to study the word of God, and find out where I belong in the plan of God for my very own life. So I began to face the truth and the truth has set me free. The title of my poem is MAY I HAVE THIS DANCE.

MAY I HAVE THIS DANCE

Living in this world full of troubles and strife
You may have to dance to the beat of life
No matter what the circumstance or the price
You haven't danced until you can
Pop your fingers and clap your hands
Swing your hips and move your feet
In the face of your old enemy
You have to live life one step at a time
Dance to the beat at all times
Good times bad times, what ever
You must keep dancing and be very prayerful
Pray when you feel like it
And pray when you don't
Prayer is the first step you see
To Jesus prayer is like a sweet melody
You really haven't danced yet you see
It's only when you can dance in the face of your enemy
The enemy must first be clearly revealed
It could be in your heart deeply concealed
No matter what you may think or how one may feel
Facing the enemy is the real deal
But be not deceived and misled too
The real enemy could very well be you
Where is the enemy of your life
Could it be pain, fear, envy or strife
You have not danced until you can
Prance upon the inner man, I say prance upon the inner man
When you can look inside yourself
And except your bad as well as your best
No matter how bad your best may be
You can began to step on that old enemy

A dance does not have to include another partner
There comes a time when you must dance with yourself and no other
When you conquer or overcome the faults within
Then you can become your very own best friend
You can rejoice and give thanks as you lift your feet
To dance on that old enemy
<u>When you can love those who has done you wrong</u>
Greet them with a smile as the beat goes on
You may dance to beat of life as you stand
Look yourself in the mirror and say
May I have this dance?

<u>When you can reflect on the road that you have traveled</u>
Realize the bad in your life only helped to make you better
You can dance to the beat of life forever and ever
So what if you have a partner or not
You can rejoice, give thanks and still praise your God
May I have this dance you can say to yourself
When you realize both you and your enemy
Only helped to make you better

<u>When you have been raped by ignorance</u>
And robbed by rebellion
Then you realize it was only, BY GODS GRACE, that you truly got better
Surely you can dance alone, forever and ever

No matter where you find yourself in life
You must understand, God sent his son as a sacrifice
So a partner is not a must you see
Tell yourself, I will dance with me

MAY I HAVE THIS DANCE

Dance on the problem
Dance on the promise, he promised never to leave
All we have to do is believe
Dance to the beat of life
God has truly paid a great price
So that you and I can enjoy this life

<u>Why don't you get those shackles off your feet?</u>
Go ahead clap those hands and praise God please
Get up out of your condition and dance to the beat
It makes no difference whether or not I have a partner you see
I have been washed in the blood and my Lord and Savior is with me
PARDON ME SATAN
<u>I got a reason to dance: excuse me, no thank you; I will dance with me</u>
No I am not asking for a partner you see
I will just pop my fingers and move my feet
And I: Oh Yes : I will dance with me
AND SO I SAY TO MYSELF
May I have this dance as I look to the FATHER
May I have this dance as I yield to the SON
May I have this dance as I bow to the HOLY ONE
MAY I HAVE THIS DANCE.

MY LITTLE ANGELS

There two very special angels in my life
One of them is seven and the other one's five
They are very precious to me, oh so dear
I love to call them and keep them near
They are very very close to my heart
Everyday for them I say thank you God
Just being able to see the sparkle in their eyes
Brings me great Joy makes me smile when I want to cry
My little angels came in the form of my granddaughters
God made them precious and to me they are flawless
Grandma may sound like I am bragging a little
That is exactly the case this is not a riddle
Yes my angels are very important, in case you are curious
I Love them a lot and I am serious
Chelsea and Brittany is their names
They are grannies angels and that's no game
My Little Angels sets off a flame *********
Of course by now time has gone by
They will always be my angels no matter how time flies
Before I know it they will soon be grown
But the sparkle in their eyes makes my heart their home
In my heart my Angels will forever live on

REAL LOVE CAN'T DIE

I sometimes have wondered and ask myself why
Honey do you laugh, when you suppose to cry
There are painful memories, and brutal things
That really should cause me to cry but instead I sing

Jesus loves me this I know because the bible tells me so
This is a song I had to learn as a little girl
But little did I know, God truly controls the world
I use to sing that song like a little mocking bird
Sometimes I would hum it until I found the words

I remember walking to church for many years
I watch the saints, shout for joy, pray and shed tears
I really didn't know what all of that meant
When mom said let's go to church, Uh I just went

Yes I went to church but I didn't know God
I knew that for us times was really really hard
The feeling I got in church as a little girl was good
Although I really didn't know, God like I should

Oh but as life kept introducing itself to me
The more I realized, there is a God that I cannot see
But no matter what , I will bend my knees
I thought this is just simply the way it has got to be
So every night on the floor I would go
To pray to a God I really didn't know

I found out as time went on
Jesus never no never leaves me alone
I also learned that he died
Suffered much pain and sometimes cried

But then I heard he rose again
With all power in his hand

He has the power to do all things
He even has to power to give me wings
In my spirit I began to fly
High above all those who had fed me lies

I've had people to tell me they love me
And in my heart, if they said it I believed
But they really wanted me to die
They enjoyed removing my smile
And would rather see me cry

I really use to be so hurt by folk
Because this man called God I really didn't know
I had no idea he died for me
Then he rose again just to set me free

He died to set me free from all enemies
He even opens my eyes and freed me from me
I found out through the years, there is no greater love
Than the Love of my lord and savior who was sent from above

I found out Jesus could not be killed
And he wouldn't even die
Because he had not only me but you on his mind
No matter whether I meet an enemy or a friend
I will always smile and look to heaven until the end

I realize now there is no need to hate or even cry
Cause you can't kill love
Haven't you heard real love will rise?
Jesus has proved it, and it is no surprise
All of our needs he will supply
Please you must trust Jesus
Because real love can't die

PHYSICAL VS. SPIRITUAL

You don't want to get Physical
Cause I love being Spiritual
Your intellectuality
Can't touch my inner ability

You see I use to be filled with vulnerability
Cause I really didn't know that much about me
Till one a day a man touch me, whose name is Holy
He showed me some things I couldn't even see
Until the Holy Spirit start operating within me

So getting Physical is no longer a thrill to me
I have learned to be pure in my sexuality
No longer cling to that flexibility
So if you want to love me it's not your touch that thrills
First you must connect with my man: so you can feel what I feel

So your sexuality, personality, intellectuality, and your ability
To be as cool and calm, and collective as can be
I'm sorry it doesn't do a thing for me
You see I've gain a new versatility
And now the touch is within me
Its called Spirituality
Can you feel me?

Oops I'm sorry you can't touch this
The feeling I'm speaking of is not physical
So come on baby let's get Spiritual
Don't want to lay with you, I just want to Pray with you
Don't' want to fight with you, please let me unite with you
Don't want to hate on you, I just want to love you
I ain't mad at you boo; I just got heaven in my view

This is not just some cute words or just another lyric
My man named Holy, designed this in the spirit
Not Physical to Physical, nor is it analytical
So come on baby let's get Spiritual
The touch that we need ultimately
Is not a touch that the natural eye can see
It has to come from deep within you and me
It's called my Spirituality
Now I'll ask the Question again
CAN YOU FEEL ME MY FRIEND
Because this is the way it's got to be

Physical vs. Spirituality

TO HATE MY SISTER IS TO HATE MYSELF

I am sick and tired of some of us sick sisters
Sitting right in the church house telling God that we love him
Knowing deep in your heart you are telling lies
You are looking at a sister whom you just despise

You think you are keeping it all in disguise
God knows your heart and he hears your lies
You put on this cute little fake crisp smile
Knowing that you hate her all the while

Oh did I say hate perhaps I did
There use to be a time when I would be afraid
To tell the truth about all of this cute little fake stuff
I am not afraid anymore because in God I trust

Yes I trust God and I Love him too
So I don't have to be afraid of you you and you
I can stand boldly and tell the truth
How can I love God and hate you too

To Love you my sister is to love myself
When I don't feel that I can love you, I call upon God for his help
Since we are the work of his mighty creation
Then he only sees his loving spirit and not our faces

So when I feel in my heart that I do not love you
Pride has no place in my heart, I know what to do
I call on God for his love is true
I can't love me if I can't love you

This may be a little touchy for some of you
Just please remember I ain't mad at you boo
I got to love you, because I've got heaven in my view
So if you say you love God you got to love me too
Cause God made me a part of you
Like an expert seamstress who hits every stitch
God created us in one spirit
That spirit was sent from heaven above
That spirit my sister is called love

No God truly is not looking at our figure eight
Nor does he see our pretty little faces
He only adores and adorns what he has made
When he see us loving and living in his grace
Letting him know that we do appreciate
All of his mighty mighty creations
So don't hate me sister or anyone else
Remember to hate my sister is to hate myself
Again I ain't mad at you boo
I just got heaven in my view
And Gods love inside of me holds better than super glue
I can trust him at his word because his word is true
And you can't stop me from loving you

WHEN YOU STOP LOVING YOU

No greater love than a man to lay down his life
Is some sacred words spoken by Jesus Christ
He wasn't selfish or anything
He was laying down his life for his friends

Although he gave his life for all to receive
There are many who absolutely refuse to believe
So instead of being thankful and gratifying
Some ungrateful folks yelled crucify him

What does that mean to you and me?
It means Jesus Christ died to set us free
He is love if we will just only believe
Love is for all, and even the blind can see

But I thought about something very seriously
It is a dangerous thing to stop loving me
When I refuse to seek the creator of my soul
I began to walk in places that I do not know

I follow this one and that one to no end
Trusting not in God but believing my friends
I end up with pain and disappointment over and over again
Because I looked for love in the wrong places from the beginning

Finally life's turmoil's lead me to a place
Where I wanted to see God face to face
Since the word was the only best thing
I decided to trust it and see what it would bring

It didn't take several days no only a few

For me to realize that Gods word really is true
If I wanted to find peace and learn what to do
I had to tell myself, honey you have got to love you

You cannot find it anywhere else
God gives his word and his spirit to enable you to love yourself
This old mean world can be very cruel honey its true
But the most dangerous thing is when you stop loving you

WHAT ABOUT ME

You made me cute for all to see
But deep inside, I wonder what about me
I was very empty spiritually
Because in my home was only brutality
So fear and pain has taken a hold on me

To the outside world, physically
I was so cute and dressed as pretty as can be
But I am filled with so much pain and misery
And I am left with the question, what about me

The clothes look good and my hair does too
But deep inside, I am torn in too
So everyone looks at me and say how cute is she
But no one can see the scars and bruises inside of me
I'm so full of wounds internally

What about me I'm trapped in a war oh my God?
The war in my home that's now seeping into my heart
The outside of me is what they see
But the inside of me is suffering
From a lack of peace, love and affection and no direction
But these needs goes un-noticed cause they just look at my clothes and
My cute little shoes, and my hair especially
While the inside of me is crying please, please ,please
What about Me
My heart is bruised my mind is confused
What about Me
Forget the dog gone brand new shoes
What about Me

Can't feel that fancy hair do
What about Me
You treat each other extremely cruel
<u>What you want is all that you see</u>
But I want to know WHAT ABOUT ME

WHEN YOU SHOT MY MOMMY

When you shot my mommy you shot me too
I was not just a part of my mommy
But a part of you

I am just a very little girl
You have already began to shatter my world
My little mind is very photogenic
I am not really sure that I can forget it

I saw you shoot my mommy on that day
Then the police officer took me away
Although I was removed from the scene
The gunshot, the screams, and the blood it all stayed with me

It was in my mind when I went to sleep
I was tossing in turning because mommy was bothering me
I kept hearing her scream and cry for her life
And So I tossed and I turned all through the night

Why did you hurt her daddy and me too?
I want to love you daddy but I am afraid of you
I am not just a part of her but a part of you too
I am caught between love and fear I don't know what to do

Will you love me daddy or hurt me too
You are called my daddy but I am afraid of you
She took the bullet
But I'm feeling the wounds
Because when you shot mommy you shot me too
Now tell me what is a little girl suppose to do

Because when you shot mommy you shot me too
Now I am left feeling so confused
Because when you shot mommy you shot me too

WHO AM I

Born into a place called earth in a sinful world
Many years ago my mother delivered a baby girl
A little girl given the name called Phyllis
Born into a world so full of filthiness

The one thing about this that seriously concerns me
Is that among all this filth there is still some beauty
Living in this world full of troubles and strife
Just living, life itself adds beauty to life

Sometimes I do wonder Who Am I
These words to my lord and savior I cry
Because I don't know who I really am
I ask my Father God to guide me and hold my hand

Sure my mother gave birth to a little girl
But can she tell me who she brought into this world
Yes a little girl with out a choice but to be born into sin
Whose body needs to be washed all over again?

Water washes the flesh that's understood
If my heart is to be cleaned it must be by the blood
The blood of Jesus or some says the blood of the lamb
Only cleansing me with his blood, will define who I am

I love my mother and I thank you very much ma'am
But only Gods son can tell me who I really am
I saw mom kneel to pray and sometimes she wept
I thank God for her prayers and for my life he has kept
This little girl has now learned to pray for myself

I realize I needed to have my sins washed away
Belief in my heavenly Father from day to day
He has shown me that I am his queen
So from now on Jesus name I'll sing
Throughout all of eternity
Thank you Father God theses words I cry
Keep leading and guiding me and tell me who am I

WHAT LANGUAGE DO YOU SPEAK

I learned a great lesson in life you see
While inviting someone into my home who was not like me
She was a different color and a different culture too
We spent a couple of weeks together and somehow we made it through

We even had total different languages we spoke
What she was saying to me wow I didn't know
Same thing with her when I spoke she just smiled
We figured it out somehow after a while

Although her language to me was never understood
I am sure my language to her was just as confusing
She had a little child that was terminally ill
But somehow I was able to help administer every pill
To help this young mother nurture her sick child
We both would give signs as we nurtured her and smiled

Sometimes we would try to communicate with one another
We would just fall out with laughter while one tried to understand the other
As the days went by we began to understand the language
We developed a love that erased all barriers

She couldn't speak English and I couldn't speak Spanish
But by time she left one thing I began to understand and
The greatest lesson which was learned over and above
Is that the greatest language is the language of love
So as you travel through life this week
Why don't you think about what languages do you speak

Everyone understands kindness and love

IT'S A NEW DAY

Everyday of life is a brand new day
A day of which one have never seen
So what does a new day really mean

A new day may be the best day of the rest of your life
When we really deal with the struggles and strife
Sometimes we can't tell if it's day or night
The more we live the more we have to fight

We fight sometimes about battles that are not ours
We sometimes realize that we are somewhat powerless
So we become exhausted with fighting ignorance
Fighting about sex, race, all kinds of things which doesn't make any sense
There are certainly much more important ways our time could be spent

So we can decide at any given moment to turn another way
Let those who choose to embrace ignorance fight on as I pray
Seek God and thank God for my mind being illuminated
Allowing me to realize that the battle is not mine anyway
So I will let those that enjoy the fight have my little space
And tomorrow for me it's a brand new day

I DO NOT KNOW STABILITY

The ways of stability I do not know
So I grab my little bag and I'm ready to go
Yes my bag is always packed and ready
Cause my little life is so unsteady

I'll go with anyone that will take me
Cause my parents hasn't taught me stability
Nor have they even considered the danger you see
So I'm free to go with anyone I please

Morality, security reality and stability
In my life is far fetched as can be
My life may be filled with insecurity
Because I'm allowed to live dangerously

I didn't have any choice in the matter
I was conceived by careless parents, made possible by the master
My parents was only thinking of self pleasure you see
But in the process of pleasure they made me

Now that I'm here their selfishness is clear
That's why they really have no fear
Of what's happens to me or how I live

They only cares about themselves and how they feel
Constantly pleasing flesh and seeking thrills
Therefore they don't even desire the ability
To teach me morals, strength and stability

So I am free to grab my little bags and go
Here there and everywhere you know

I am probably one of many you see
That's why our youth are living so dangerously

Not to mention some who are living in the street
Because there is no home life and no stability
So we are forced to live, a life that's devastating
Cause me and my parents are not relating
We are complete strangers there's no communication

I'm just a child and I'm not capable
Of leading life that's safe and stable
I'll follow anyone who leads me
Excepting and trying to follow, whatever they want to teach
I have no idea where this life leads
Maybe Gods angel will watch over me
Because I am too young to even see
The danger that lies ahead of me
Because I do not know stability

I hope someone will pray for me
As I go traveling here and there you see
Neither my parents nor me know stability
And prayer is the only protection for me
Do you have time or availability?
To use the faith that it takes for me
Prayer and faith is the key
Because I do not know stability

HAVE YOU EVER BEEN TO CHURCH

Ever been to church and they were preaching on heaven above
But you didn't feel welcome and you felt no love
You wonder if this is spirituality
Or if this is just a formality

You know when real love is being displayed
I often say real love can truly be felt
And it certainly cannot be faked
No matter how well one speak or what they say
Love can be felt and will not leave you dismayed

I'm talking about that agape love
That kind that loves in spite of
In spite of my faults and my short comings
In spite of your approval or anyone's

Only Gods Love makes everyone feel
Welcome and Loved cause his love is real
He does not love me or you because of
Honey He loves us in spite of

Because he understood why he was sent
He stood faithful and he represents
God the father, cause he is his son
Jesus knows that they two are one
He was not a lip server, he lived it
He knew he was one but three in the spirit

Ever been to church and you felt disconnected
Perhaps because Love has not been perfected
Maybe the words from their lips was infected

With a form of godliness and not real affection

Ever been to church and every word you heard
Really convinced you that Jesus is the word
Well if the word of God has not been made clear to you
Let me assure you that Gods word is true
God is Love and he really really love me and you
If you ever been to church and heard the real truth
Then you understand that the real church is you

Have Ever Been To Church

WHAT WILL YOU DO

I've often heard my father say
The most powerful words that still rings from his grave
It takes me six months to mind my own business
And six months to leave yours alone
And by the time these months roll around all my time is gone
Just when I arise to possibly start to meddling
The time starts all over again

So unless you are going to be a help to someone
There is not much time to meddle or become
Busy taking care of other folks business
For you will have to look at your time clock and get with it
For too much time has passed and your own business is not fixed

I thought about that as I began to grow up and become independent
Minding your own business is some time well spent
For if you don't take care of your own matters
Then who else will look after
What's important to you
What will you do

I CHOOSE YOU

When growing up as a young child in school
There seems to be so much for my little body to do
Teachers, principles, mom, dad, and classmates too
I have to choose friends and some times kids are so cruel

I really had not thought about what's important to me
Because I'm young and I can't define much of anything
What's the definition of friend honey
To me it is fun, laughter, and who plays with me

I really don't know that much about me
So choosing friends, is just not that serious you see
So good habits, bad habits who cares what ever
Everybody is my friend, forever and ever

This is what my elementary mind says
But as I grow up and follow some of their ways
I find myself getting in trouble almost every day
At least with my parents and the teachers anyway
Why because I follow my friends and do not obey

In most cases it was my friends that were the blame
But I still got the punishment just the same
Well shucks, I'm tired of this mess, I know what to do
When it comes to real friends
I am going to take a long hard look in my mirror and say
I CHOOSE YOU
When traveling the road of life in the end
You had better learn to become your own best friend

CLASS-ROOM CLOWNS

Class room clown is a dangerous place to be
One reason I say this specifically
Because no education can limit your desires and your dreams
Interfere with you becoming what you want to be
And having no education is not very funny

Sometimes young kids like to make everyone laugh
So they become the head clown of their class
Not realizing what danger that they are in
Education is no joke you must study to win

Class rooms clown find out in the end
That making folk laugh didn't gain you friends
Because when grading time came they wanted to win
You are left possibly being the failure in the end

Not prepared for college or even technical school
All because you clowned, laughed and broke all the rules
Maybe you thought you were being real cool
Now you are left feeling alone and miss-used

Oh yes education sometimes play a big part
In how people treat you and sometimes it is very hard
To get the respect from those who feel you don't know
So you find out you were the clown but they run the show
I'd like to say as I bring this poem to and end
Please don't be a Class room clown my friends

I CAN

Life is not race but it is a journey
Every thing you have you must earn it
Whether you are a mere woman , child or man
If you want to win, you must say I can

Words alone have so much power
Jesus said let there be a night and day
Just think without these words there wouldn't be hours
When Jesus created Life a day and a night
He didn't stop he said let there be light

That's what the whole world needs to see
There is power in what you say if you can only believe
Can you believe, Oh yes you can
Stop singing you can't and obey Gods commands

I can do all things through Christ who strengthens me
I can be anything God wants me to be
Yes my features, my views are different from you
My resources may seem limited too, but faith tells me I can
AND SO CAN YOU

I will walk by faith and not by sight
Praise my God both day and night
Since he gave me life , yes he gave it all
So whatever I need on him I call

He always answers no matter what the request
God always grants me with his very best
He is great, he is almighty, he is a faithful man

I 've never heard him say I can't , It is always I can
This should be the Song of every boy girl woman or man
Don't Say I can't you must say I CAN

CHILD ABUSE

Have you ever in your life heard of so much abuse
Especially among the innocent our youth
When I speak of youth it is not by age
Youthfulness in the spirit the mind and all kind of ways
There are people of age who have lived many years
Who is affected by abuse and they are still shedding tears
From some cruel things that happen along time ago
So they kept the pain hidden because they wanted no one to know

So the young the old the poor and the rich
In some way another have possibly been hit
With blows of disappointment and unkind acts
Abuse is very destructive and that's a fact

So now we have a society of people
Who looks well on the outside but the inside is bleeding
Yes they are shedding invisible blood like rivers of sweat
No one seem to have noticed it yet
That there are some old wounds you will never forget
Your smile is not filled with true happiness
The smile just tries to cover hurt, shame and regrets

Regrets, about what life has done
Forgetting that the battle has been fought and the victory has been won
When God sent his only begotten son
He died not only for your abuse but for everyone
So don't feel like you have been forsaken
God has a blessing for you in the making
Jesus was the first to experience abuse
He didn't murmur complain or make any excuse

He was treated cruel and he was false accused
He took an unjust beating and died not for a few
He took the abuse for everyone including me and you
I know it may have hurt you for the things they took you through
But please remember Mary's baby was the very first child abused
He went through all of the suffering so we could get through

Every bit of pain suffered from child abuse

BECAUSE YOU KNOW NOT WHO YOU SIT AMONG

So you think you sitting here with me
But you are actually sitting among three
The Father, son and Holy Spirit honey you see
All three in one is living inside me

Greater is he that is in me, than he that is in the world
The greater one within me is my lord and savior whose name is Jesus
I am committed to living a life that will constantly please him
Satan tried to kill him but the power of the spirit is what kept him living

Because he rose on the third day with all power in his hand
His spirit was released to every woman and man
There is no respecter of persons I understand
Anyone can be filled with this spirit didn't you know
Even the little children can receive the spirit and grow

I am grateful that Jesus died to set us all free
He died to free anyone who chooses to be
He sent obedience and love wrapped in flesh you see
He did not send him alone ,there was actually three
The father son and Holy Spirit from heaven to earth he came
That is why there is so much power in Jesus Name

That same power is living in all believers today
It is given to those who lives according to what he say
It is given to those who call on his precious name
It is given to those who humble themselves and pray
It is given to those who practice living the righteous way

This relationship is a very sacred one
You see some folks don't have a clue where you came from

So they disrespect you and cannot see the holy one
That lives inside, all three and then some
They fail to recognize that you are anointed
Not to mention you have been appointed
So it is easy for them to do you wrong
Because they do not know who they sit among

The bible declares I shall do greater works
So I hold fast to my faith, and I am not easily hurt
By what I hear, or what you do wrong
Because you know not who you sit among

You look in my face and you think it is just me you see
I'm sorry to disappoint you friend there are actually three
The father, son, and Holy Spirit living inside of me
Just delighting in opportunities to set you free
I will pray and praise him all the day long
I will greet you with love and smile a as I sing my song
I have no time to focus on what you've done wrong
This is my story, this is my song
I will praise my savior all the day long
Because you know not who you sit among

AND SO SHE CRIES

This is one of the most important pieces of poetry
It is a very sensitive true and heartfelt story
There was a little girl who lives in a very confused world
The one thought that won't leave me alone
Is that there is lots of confusion in a place called home?

I can relate to this child's feelings you see
Because that little child use to be me
No peace No peace and then no peace
Is this the way home is suppose to be

There was one thing this child said to me
Sometimes it even disturbs my sleep
When ask why she was failing in pre- school
She explained from a child's mind in just a moment or two

There's is this little girl that torments her and won't let her sleep
No one will listen so she just weeps
Can't function in school for her brain thinks in three parts
Concentrating in the class room is extremely hard

Because she says one part of my brain is thinking about class
The other part of my brain thinks of this child that torments me
every chance she gets
The middle of my brain she says is thinking about God
Man this was some chilling words to my ears, listening was really hard
From the mouth of a child but the mind of God
When I heard her speak this was my first thought

When it's time to go home now she becomes really sad
Not wanting to go home because conditions are really bad

No one listens to me she says and they are telling lies
Nothing she can do and so she cries

I believe her cry is just one of many
Little children who is neglected, abandoned, abused and innocent
Cannot take care of themselves don't know how to survive?
Caught up in a web of mass confusion, insensitive humans, and lies
Too young to fight, too tender eyesight and so she cries
Wanting a way out but there is no where to go
And she has no choice in the matter you know
I believe this is a cry to us all
Can we continue to allow our youth to fall?
And so she cries
And so she cries

LIKE THE BIRDS I SING

I awakened in the stillness of the night
When everything was solemn and quiet
Never really paid to much attention
To the melody of the birds not to mention
The fact that I really didn't know
That the birds are not on a time schedule so
No matter what time of day or night
Those little birds always have a song that's right
For any occasion no matter whether it is day or night

So like the bird I want to sing
No matter what the day may bring
It may be sunshine or it may be rain
It could be brightness or the darkest hour
There should be a melody sung to he who gives us power
To get up and get started for the day
We should sing praises to God always
For it is he who created us and not we ourselves
Like the faithful bird I wish to give him all that I have
The bird only has a chirp and a melody to sing
They don't need to have a schedule, to be prompted or anything
They gladly use what they have and so they sing

When you wake up through the night just listen if you will
They give God all that he gave them to give
No matter what time of day or night
They praise God all the time just check them out
So I say to you no matter what life brings
Look up to heaven and say like the birds I will sing

THAT'S NOT WHO I AM

The bible tells me that I am marvelously and wonderfully made
In the image of God , I was created
But this journey of life must be lived
Everyday trying to fulfill Gods will

So while I travel down life's highway
There have been some terrible mistakes I've made
I have been done wrong and I have also done wrong
Found friends for life and then lost some

Some I unwillingly betrayed, but I told them the truth
Thinking that the truth would keep us connected and take us through
Any hard time difficulty or challenge we would face
But my friend pulled out an eternal eraser

Erased me instantly, would not forgive
I was truly hurt about all of this
I was stuck on pause and a lot of guilt
But finally I realized I must live

Friendship is not bonded until it's been tested
So I guess the test was to let me see
That our friendship really wasn't what it was suppose to be
Maybe just maybe, it was never meant to be

So mistakes never forgiven by so called friends
But God will forgive me over and over again
Yes I did do some things that were not to pleasing
But my heart is extremely remorseful, you must believe me
So I wonder will God forgive you and give you another chance

Because that's what I did but that's not who I am

I am weak but God is strong
He knows who and where I belong
So I am not what you think of me
I am being conformed into what God wants me to be
Yes sir and thank you ma'am
That's what I did but that's not who I am

AND NOW I LIVE

A baby is not considered alive until you hear him cry
A man does not know life until he first dies
A bird doesn't know height until he first flies
Before the sun sets it must first rise

Why don't you rise up and began to live
Why are you searching for a cheap thrill
Why do you seek only for what you can feel
Why are you constantly getting , but never gives
Unless your unsuspecting motive is being fulfilled

We reach and grab for things to bring us happiness
Sometimes stepping on others trying to reach a level of success
While we are racing through life lanes at our best
We find our self on highway distress

Now that the ladder of life has you at it's peak
You realize maybe this is not all it is cracked up to be
You thought every thing you needed was in your degree
Or perhaps fine women or men would be all you would ever need
And oh don't let me forget the material things
You have now found the American dream
Wasn't thinking about salvation although it is free

Now suddenly everything began to slowly change
You find out like a sport, life is a real tough game
Job has crashed, sometimes family, friends, lovers gone, whose the blame
You find yourself struggling to call on Jesus Name
No need to let pride bring about shame
God is always the same he never changes
He loves you just the same

You almost gave all that you had to give
Only for a false sense of Joy and a dissolving thrill
Almost everything you acquired dissolved like a pill
It doesn't matter what place time or day
God will always hear you when you pray
God makes promises that he will fulfill
He stretches forth his hand as you do his will
When others leave he'll be by your side to forgive
It is then you pause and say and now I live

CROSS BURNERS

In America we have cross burners with hidden faces
Using scare tactics for another race and
I saw a Caucasian on the television crying
Said he felt pain for the African American

You know what I am a sister it is true
My goodness I feel pain for African Americans too
It is not the cross that is killing us boo
It is the self hatred that I think is so cruel

So cross burners, burn your cross that's no problem
Killing and dying is a easy solution to this please help us
Have you not noticed that killers are very active?
Some are even experts and they need no practice

If you are bold enough to burn
Then be bold enough to learn
That hating takes on a boomerang effect
What you throw out there, is what will come back

Oh yeah it will hit you one day right in the face
Not from a foreigner but from your own precious race
That little child's mind you have poisoned for so long
Who is bombarded with bitterness, and doesn't know right from wrong
Struggling in his or her mind, as you sing those hate songs

Like the Mississippi burning, three little black girls died
For many many years their black mothers cried
The cold hearted killer, his face he did hide
But suddenly his own grand daughter couldn't keep it inside

So what did she do, she turned grand papa in
She was a little child that heard every word he had said
Oh he celebrated how he roasted those blacks
He failed to realize the one devastating fact
That one day his hate and lies would all come back

Not from the blacks or any other race
In that court room of justice, he stared his own grand child in the face
Oops I am sure for just a little bit it must to have hurt
Just like he felt about blacks, he must to have felt just like dirt
This ought to be a very strong lesson to learn
You only spook yourself, so let the cross burn baby burn

Finally I will say
Cross burners should become cross learners
There are not very many slave runners
There is a cross still left for all sinners
Jesus Christ is a powerful soul winner
So cross burners why don't you make his day?
Repent, become godly sorry ask for forgiveness and pray

FASTING AND PRAYING

Fasting and praying and praying and fasting
Fasting and praying and praying and fasting
Hoping my life will continue to last and
I can tell people the truth about what my God can do

I've had so many enemies and fake friends too
That tried so hard to persuade me to break all the rules
I know my God tells me to love everyone
Love is much more powerful than a loaded gun

I had not one but several boyfriends
They told me they loved me and I said I love you
My little heart was so sincere, I was telling the truth
I love them so much I didn't know what to do

Didn't take but a little time in the relationship
Before I found out they was just shooting from the lip
They didn't mean a single word they said
They was telling lies and just messing with the little brain in my head
All those lies just so they could only get me in bed

So now after I find out the real truth
My little heart is torn right in to
My head is hurting and my mind is spinning
I have laid down my body and I have been sinning
With folk who has been lying straight from the beginning
I can't take this I just want to end it
All
Oh my God I feel like dying
My pillow is soaking wet from all this crying

I know what I have been taught in my church days
I am suppose to love everybody and never hate
But right now I can't see, I can't hear, I can't fake
I planning to put something on somebody's plate

So I rise from my pillow of tears, hurt and pain
My mind is all twisting and I'm going in sane
Hating this person because they are the blame
For me feeling all this hate, hurt and pain
So now I want him to feel what I feel
I began to think and take a chill pill

I must calm myself down and try to think clear
Cause I want to take somebody out of here
I had so much hate and very little love
I wanted to pay him for what he had done

So while making plans to repay this man
Instead of getting the bible in my hands
I went to the store to purchase me a friend
This friend is known as a four hundred and ten

Hold on I'm not going to leave you hanging
Give me a second and I will explain this
You see four hundred and ten is a shot gun
I was going to kill someone and have me some fun

I thought it would do my heart good to see him die
For all those lies he told me, and made me cry
To see him die would only make me smile I thought
But I had to suddenly put my brain on halt

Then I thought to kill him, will be to kill me too
Because I've got two precious girls that I just might lose
All because I lost my mind, and gave my heart to this fool
Then I began to think, Oh man now what else can I do
Every thought I had was breaking Gods rules

So now that my mind has become unraveled
My heart has settled down and my eyes are drying
Yes tears have ran dry and I can't keep on crying
About a person who doesn't even love himself
At that point I realized we both needed help

He couldn't help me an I couldn't help him
So I decided to return to God again
I started going to church and listening intensely
I needed some help and I wanted some relief
The kind of love that some men have to give
Was about to cause me to self destruct, but I decided to live

So the preacher was preaching real real good
I heard him clearly and for the first time I understood
That my body was a temple and it belonged to God
So I start turning away from my old ways and it was kind of hard

But one day I heard that some things come only by Fasting and praying
Ah that's my answer I thought, so my heart start saying
Yes it was the strangest thing; for the first time my heart was talking to me
It said girl don't be to proud try it, Fast pray and bend them knees
And you will see

So I began to listen to my heart
I got down on my knees to make a new start
God took my hand, and held it gently
His word and his spirit filled me with so much peace
I actually was learning how to love me

So then I took it a step further
Cause what the preacher was saying I really heard it
Fast and pray, and pray and fast
Just let the lord Jesus erase your past
I now have more Joy, peace and love than I've ever had

After being delivered and set free
I was able to lead this man to my Jesus, one day long afterwards in the street
He didn't even bother to ask me about me
He said you have been with Jesus, I can see
But that only came because I stayed on my bending knees
God gave me peace like I could not believe
He has truly truly set me free
I can now love like it suppose to be

So I have been fasting and praying and praying and fasting
So that I can tell you the truth
About not myself, but what my God can do
What he did for me honey he can also do for you

LOVE ISN'T LOVE

Love isn't love until you learn to love you
Without God that is kind of hard to do
God is Love and he defines it to
Any other kind of love is false and untrue
False love will leave you feeling blue
Oh honey please without God you don't have a clue

Oh yeah if you're lucky you can get a good feeling sometimes
From someone who's an expert with words, that will just blow your mind
Oh but honey as life and time goes on
If there's no love of God in them, you will be soon left alone
Wondering what in the world have I done wrong?

Love isn't love because you went to bed
And your heart is not whole because of what he said
Your spirit is not filled with joy and happiness
When you thought the love making was the best
Actually another can't give you what they didn't get

You see there's no greater love than a man who lay down his life for his friends
That is what the son of God, whose name is Jesus actually did
Unless a person is filled with the true spirit of God
Loving you or themselves will be very hard

So stop looking for love everywhere else
Honey you will have to learn how to love yourself
Just calm down and stop, ask God for his help
Cause Love isn't love until
You can love yourself

I KNOW HOW TO GO ON THE DOWN LOW

I am just as much woman
As you are a man
But there is one thing darling I do understand
And that is God created me to hold your hand
This is not just a wish but Gods command

He wishes above all things that my soul would prosper
I know that to prosper I must be in order
Follow the plan that God has made
I will follow you as you listen to God and obey

As long as you let God lead the way
In obedience to God, Honey I know my place
So I will follow you as God leads the way
Because as you follow him, I won't be lead astray

Before I met you I have always prayed
Because the world was leading me in the wrong way
So I stopped, looked, and listen to what God has to say
Now I am being guided down a street called straight

So if you want to play games and not be straight
Maybe you should find someone else to play
There is nothing you can hide from me when I pray
My God is always on time an not a moment too late

I am not desperate to get involved with people you know
I just watch patiently and pray, and I take it real slow
So please don't try to rush me, or play games as we go
Cause honey like some I too know how to go on the down low
Let's be real how low can you go

UNIDENTIFIED HEROES

There are many fine people that I know
That is real true living heroes
Although their names no one will ever know
Because they are not doing good just for show

A Hero that takes in a mother's child
Guide them straight for a long while
Never having any biological attachment
But filled with so much love and affection

This particular hero goes unnoticed by man
But I am so glad that God holds their hand
Sometimes others will never understand
Just how one gives so much but never take the stand

Never take the stand to be recognized
Always remaining in disguise
Never even getting a thanks much to my surprise
But I know all this is under Gods watchful eye

An unidentified hero plays such a great part in our society
Without them some people would be doomed actually
Because much of the time this hero takes care of those
That everyone else don't even care to know
So I thank God for unidentified heroes

LET MY HEART GO

I was thinking about life's winding road
How we enter into this world and then we must go
To a place for most of the living that is unknown
It is a place called heaven where God sits on a throne

So in order to get there we must work for a crown
We are born into a world full of life's ups and downs
There are instructions that we must follow in this life
Even though we are in the midst of wars, troubles and strife

God ask us to surrender our hearts to him
So he can lead us and guide us safely in
Into a place that he has prepared
A place where he and his son Jesus shares

We are to surrender our hearts to God
In the midst of this corrupt world, and it seems so hard
We didn't do anything but be born right from the start
And the evil one already has a grip on our hearts

We are all born into this sinful world
Make no difference whether you are a boy or a girl
This thing called life is a mystery
Only God himself knows what's best for me

So we sometimes get started on a wrong path you know
We place our trust and our hearts in the wrong folks
Then somehow you realize you are on the wrong road
Then you cry out to God tell them to let my heart go

SINGLE PARENTS

Single parents have an awesome task
Most of the time they just have to react
No time to stop and ask questions why
For fear of wasting time and the children may die

Maybe not an actual physical death
But die spiritually from not getting just the basic help
Someone has to feed them and supply a shelter
In a lot of cases dad is around never
So if the family is to survive then she knows somebody better
So Mom takes on a double roll and decides it's got to be now or never

No No No No time to waste, no time to complain
Because there are mouths to be fed and bills are still rolling just the same
Even if one decided to place the blame
Hunger, hurt, insecurity has no name
So what would you say to hunger?
You are hungry because of a whoremonger
I don't think that would feel and empty stomach
So no need to even bother complaining honey

So now that we are here someone must strive
To fight and thrive to keep the family alive
Even though things are tough which is no surprise
A single parent keeps moving and keeps hope alive
That is the main key that helps her survive

Don't mean to slight the man or anything
I know for some men this is not the case

But this is one thing I will say to you
Don't expect an award for doing what you are suppose to do

Children did not ask to come here

THE HIGHER THE EAGLE FLY

I am always open to hear what wisdom has to say
This is one saying I heard from the lips of a special lady
She was a lady who loved God and she always prayed
She was willing to share anything she had on any given day

So many times my mother would seek her advice
Trying to find ways of peace for her troublesome life
This lady was someone whom you could believe
Because before she gave an answer, she'd first go on her knees

She would get her answers straight from heaven and then
If you would listen you would find peace in the end
Even if what you heard was not always good
This is something she clearly understood
So it didn't matter whether you liked it or not
If you asked the question, then the truth is what you got

So much like the eagle who flies higher than life
He soars high above all of the wicked devices
One thing this special lady told to me
Is that the higher the eagle flies the better he sees

What does this saying mean to you and me?
It means if you expect to rise above life's issues you see
You better start by bending your little precious knees
Because no one can see all of life dangers that lurks
Most every human being alive has experienced some kind of hurt
We cannot see all that God sees for us
Jesus first went down before he went up

Since God can see much more than we can
It would be wise to pray first and understand
That until we can fly in the lord
Everything else in life will just be void
So if we will go down on bending knees
We too like the eagle will be able to see
And I am sure not just maybe
May not be completely with ease
But you will fulfill your purpose and reach your destiny

WILL A REAL CHRISTIAN STAND UP

I love this lady name Mrs. Clayton
She was a woman of faith who was always praying
There was so much wisdom in what she was saying
I was a child which is so amazing
She was talking to my mother, but I got the blessing

I am so honored to have been in her presence
She lived to be one hundred and seven
I had an opportunity to learn some great lessons
Although she has passed on, she will live in my heart forever

If I never meet another real Christian in this wicked world
I am honored to say; thank God I at least met one
The love, the wisdom and knowledge I gained
Cannot be compared to any type of fame
That this world thinks it has to offer
She shared her life with Jesus and what it cost her

She had to cry sometime but she always prayed
When no one would listen to her, God heard what she said
She trusted him to make a way
So she was not ashamed to make a joyful noise as she praised
God anywhere, anytime, and she was bold and not afraid

No one ever was so bad that you had to stop loving them is what she
would say
You just keep trusting God and never cease to pray
These are the words I would hear from this precious lady
When I was just a little young tender age
I am so extremely grateful

I thank God for her labor of love
I know she is resting in heaven above
Describing this lady words, could never truly be enough
But one thing I can say, in my life she is still standing up

WHEN THE PRESSURES OF LIFE

When the pressures of life comes your way
You need to stop and think about who made the day
Have you ever thought what if God took his sun away?
Darkness and doom would be our stay, then what would you say

So if God made the day he will also make a way
If we will trust his word and obey
Call on him when we can't see our way
Keep looking forward to that brighter day

People and situations sometimes causes you to want to give up
But tell me who has authority over your life except the Lord and savior above
He not only gives us the sun light, but he also gave his son who is nothing but love
And he did not stop there he fills us with his heavenly dove
The Holy Spirit will live in every one of us
Do not forget this friend
God will live inside if you will just let him

He gave us the sun the moon the rain and the stars
God is with you wherever you are
No one can ever go so far
That God cannot reach you
He is God and there is nothing he cannot do

Your problem is his promise, he promise never to leave you
So tell me how low can you go, and what is your excuse
When the pressures of life, erases your smile in exchange for a frown
And life seems to be just pressing you down
Remember if you don't bear your cross, you get no crown

I've heard the saying
Must Jesus bear the cross alone and all the world go free?
No there is a cross for everyone and there's a cross for me
So no need to hate, hurt, wound, become self critical, self pitiful or fight
Trust Jesus to carry you through both day and night
He is waiting to give the blind their sight
Oh how wonderful to give sight to the blind
But there is nothing like illuminating the mind
Jesus truly is an everlasting light
I give you just a piece of advice
Why don't you try him and trust him with your life

HOW CAN ONE

How can one fall in love and get married
Live life as one and seem so happy
Become intimate with one another
Embrace each other as life long lovers

Then sooner a later a child may be conceived
One of the greatest miracles that could ever be
When one look at this little life put together by two human beings
As their hearts met like a meeting of a ring

There is no end and no beginning to this circle
Loving and being in love, like a unending circus
Fun, joy, rides that never come to and end
The love you have found from deep within
What a joy to have found a true friend
To call my husband my lover or my wife
To spend all of my days with for the rest of my life

Then suddenly something takes a twist
Somehow the ring of love just does not fit
The lifestyle that they once had
And now everything has gone bad
The child is no longer even a joy
And began to be treated like an object or a toy

I really want to know how can one
Connect, become mates and recreate
Another little life and then start to hate
Every thing about the child as well as their mate
And somehow this marriage becomes one's fate

Just when their life has only just begun
Suddenly something has gone terribly wrong
I love you is like a far away song
Then what do you know, another one is gone
I am left with the question, how can one

A WISE BUILDER

The word of God says he who winneth souls is wise
All of your needs he will supply
If we need help to God we must cry
He is always standing right by your side
There is no need to even think that one can hide
God breathed life into us so he is living inside

Not one living soul can abort God
It was him who created every one of us
So before we even knew that we needed a savior
He already knew because he is our creator
He knew exactly what we needed before he even made us

He knows that we all are born into sin
That's why his words tells us you must be born again
He does not have any special one's you see
Our salvation cost him, but for us it's now free
It cost Jesus much persecution, trouble and strife
And finally Jesus paid for our freedom with his life

He was sent to earth to live, teach, preach and he died
Just so not one but all of our needs would be supplied
There should be no way anyone could deny
That Jesus is always standing by our side
His love rises far above
Any type of human love

His actions supersedes all of our ways to love
They didn't take his life, he gave it up
He did all of this just to let us know
That in order to build a life, you must first let yours go

Give up, the selfish ways of thinking, to simply win a soul
Do not be ashamed of the Gospel and be bold
If you expect to consider yourself wise
Then you have to make no excuses and alibis
You must lay down your soul to win another one's life
He gave us life not to become killers
He has given his life and his word, for us to become wise builders

WHEN WE TEACH HATE

Let me give my two cents about the word hate
It is a thing that does not only separate
It also does not discriminate
It is almost like a facsimile
It looks like an untamable enemy

Sometimes we parents teach a child to hate
When we tell them bad things about our mates
Whether it is mama or daddy my friend
This thing called hate is really bad and

Especially when it is fed to a child's premature mind
Who have no idea how to internalize?
What to feel or even when to feel
Not to mention how to feel about this terrible ordeal

So if a precious little mind is taught to hate one or the other
Tell me how do they know how to separate
When and how to love, when they are filled with hate
So sooner or later it takes a boomerang effect
Because what you have given out is exactly what you get

So this is really what I am trying to say
This is a message that my heart conveyed
Is that when we teach hate
It could end up being our own fate
Because hate does not discriminate

Can't learn to hate one or some
And then suddenly love another one
Especially when it grew up in a child

Changing this issue could take a while

So my little tiny bit of advice
Would be try to spread love throughout your life
Do not allow wrong choices to promote hate
Remember if you do it could be your own fate
These are real possibilities, when we teach hate

WONDERFUL WORKERS OF GOD

Wonderful Workers of God
Originated from the heart and a simple thought
Oh how I praise God for a sincere and loving group
Trying their very best to do all they can do

Walking diligently from door to door
Determine to help everyone become restored
Restoring the minds and hearts of every lost soul
Not desiring that any be lost so we are courageous and bold

Many of us came from some really tough places
We have no fear of anyone's faces
Yes things may have been a little rough
We realized that it was actually God building us up

Therefore we walk by faith and not by sight
We pray to God both day and night
We do not fear any woman or man
We walk with God and he holds our hand

Yes there were times when life seen to have been caving in
It was only because we was not willing to give up sin
Oh but one day, we heard John say my friend
Let me tell you something, YOU MUST BE BORN AGAIN

Listen now these are some life changing words
Deep in our hearts these words did stir
Wonderful Workers individually,began to make a new start
So then we began to ignore the devils noise
Instead we stood still and heard a small still voice

It was the voice of God calling each of our names
He said listen sons and daughters today you must change
I am going to wash you all in my blood
You must seek me first is that understood

Wonderful Workers left all of the noise
Denounced sin and trusted in God
Actually we really didn't have much of a choice
Either you obey God or Life will be void
Now we work together on one accord

God has filled each of us workers with his Holy Spirit
Also filled us with some unique and wonderful gifts
We understand it's all from God and not from man
So we work together obeying Gods commands
We do sew love and we lend a hand

Wonderful Workers of God truly know
That when God calls we must go
No need to worry or try to explain
We just go take our position in Jesus Name

We are not looking for fortune nor do we want fame
How can we say thank you Jesus for all that he gave
Jesus gave his life and so much more
He gave us new life, that's why we knock on doors

Living for Christ is not a chance but it is a choice
We thank God we chose to leave all the devils noise
We took a bow face, turned to obey Gods voice
Our answer was Yes to God, Tell me what's yours

Oh hold up , you don't have to answer me
Just pray and tell God because he truly sees
You see I can watch you kneel to perhaps make that start
But Jesus see much better than me, he sees the heart
Wonderful Workers Love You and wish you much happiness

With all of our love Jesus loves you best
We say we love you as we lift up our voice
We leave with hopes that you will make God your choice
WHO WILL YOU WORK FOR
GOD or SATAN

WHO'S KNOCKING AT YOUR DOOR

The world is just filled with so much sin
I think I'll just close my door and keep mines in
Oh no as long as I am behind closed doors
Nobody but me and my sin will ever know

I will just show up at church with my nice clothes on
Sing, Shout, and Pray, and then I will go home
Yes I have paid my dues for this blessed day
Now I will go back home so I can play

My flesh says obey the word of God
But you know looking at the word for me just ain't enough
I hear this small whisper saying honey do right
But my lovers voice roars let's do it all night

So now I am torn between right and wrong
But what the heck I am at home; all locked up behind my closed doors
No body but him and me will ever really know
That nothing but sin lives behind my closed door

That little something deep inside
Keeps on telling me girl you can't hide
Oh girl would not listen so she decides
I will please my man just this one last time

Just when I was at my very weakest
A knock was at my door and it was beating
Beating so hard I started to run you see
But it was like a spirit was drawing me

I went to the door as frighten as could be, and opened the door very quickly
But the only thing there was the wind and me
My boyfriend was in the bathroom with the door closed
He shouted loudly, girl who is that knocking at your door
I said to him with tears streaming down my face
That was Jesus honey and you have got to go
And I never dealt with that sin anymore
This is the end of this piece of poetry
But I wonder if you can tell me who's knocking at your door

WHERE'S MY PEOPLE AT

Where are my people at came to me
One August morning while I was asleep
I was awakened abruptly around one fifteen
When a voice inside me began to scream

Where are my people at my dear?
A loud voice I began to hear
So I awakened quickly and grabbed my friend
One of my close friends is my little ink pen

From the tip of my pen I wrote these words
From that loud and precise voice I heard
Where my people at is what it said
Could they be rebellious and locked in a cage
Behaving like wild animals that's in rage

Where are my people at that are called by name
Are the words I continued to hear my Jesus Say
I had to stop and ask myself that question sincerely
I really truly want Gods spirit operating within me

Adam was the first human to hear these words
Why because in his life, disobedience had occurred
Adam where art thou is what Jesus asked
I am naked and ashamed was Adam's reply
These are the words that Adam cried
Cause he had disobeyed, and had no alibi

Where is my people is what he is still shouting today
Cause after all I've done for them they still won't obey
Yes where's my people at is what he's shouting today

Cause my people refuse to humble themselves and pray

I realize I must go down on bending knees
God is not asking the question
Because he is lost you see
Wheres' my people at, is asked distinctively

For the rebellious, the blind the lost, for you and for me
Through Jesus he has given both you and me, a chance to be set free
Yes Jesus gave his life for you and me, which is the ultimate key
For you and I to live this life abundantly

The key to unlock the cage that houses our mind, and perhaps the curse
He has given all of mankind the key to life, in the entire universe
That no matter where people are you see
You can be set free through Christ if you choose to be
Yes free from nakedness, sin, shame and bondage eternally
What happen to Adam no longer has to be
Jesus only came just to set us free
Jesus eyes is upon all of his creation
He recognizes that there is some like Adam still disobeying
So the question he poses, is not a fiction but a fact
Jesus really really wants to know
Where's my people at

WHERE MY STRENGTH LIES

My strength is not in my physical ability
My strength is not even in my good looks or beauty
Actually in all honesty
My strength is not really totally up to me

When you really began to face reality
Real strength comes in your ability
To acknowledge you are weak physically
And if you are going to become strong in all actuality
Then your strength will have to come through your spirituality

So to find out where our strength lies
We will have to rely on our God to supply
Everything that he wants us to be
So then we have to start with the bible you see
I am talking a life that's guided biblically
Looking to God to strengthen you and me

So my strength begins with the way I think
My strength begins when I take a drink
From the fountain of life, as I lay my life on the line
To trust God not some but all of the time
To fill me with love in my heart and wisdom in my mind

My strength must lie in my surrender to God
I realize sometimes it may seem a little hard
But if I expect to conquer and overcome my weakness
And let the devil know that he is defeated
Then I will have to bow down to my God completely

When I have accomplished this one task
Let the devil know that he has been unmasked
I know that I will gain strength and truly be blessed
I can stand tall and strong, hold my head up high
Because trusting and obeying God is where my real Strength lies

WHEN PEOPLE CARE

When people care for one another
The love is somewhat like a mother
No matter where you are or what you've done
The love and concern continues on

Whether you are near or far from home
A real love never leaves you alone
You may not even always have access to a phone
But love goes far beyond a telephone

So what I 'm really trying to say
Is that when a phone call won't work
I will always pray
Doesn't matter whether it is night or day
Prayer is more effective than a phone anyway

So Honey I love you
And I will leave it there
I will never stop sending up a prayer
God is always listening everywhere
He is not only here but he's also there
I know God truly answers prayer
When people care

WHEN I WAS

When I was a teenager
I was about to go crazy
I saw my daddy take a gunshot
By a man whom I thought liked him a lot

When I was fourteen and saw this thing happen
I couldn't understand, I was about to snap and
Suddenly curiosity kicked in
How can a man gun down his friend?

When I was so young and vulnerable you see
Not only did he shoot my dad he also shot me
Not with a four ten shot gun or any such weapon
He shattered my dreams, and clouded my endeavors

When my eyes actually were just beginning to open
I was approaching adulthood and becoming a woman
Instead of enjoying being a teenager and enjoying my friend
I had a more serious task at hand

When I was a teenager, I had to grow up kind of fast
For it look like our survival was a thing of the past
I took on the responsibility of trying to help provide
Food and shelter for my family with no time to decide

There was no time to wait to see whose job was this
I had to get busy and get a job if I wanted to live
I had no time for hesitation, I had to move quick
The job itself was not extremely hard
But my loss of youth, I felt I had been robbed

When I was a teenager I had no time to complain
I didn't have time to focus on who was the blame
So I did what I felt that I must do
I had to help my mother try to take the family through

When I was a teenager I really did not know
That what I was doing is what my God had chosen
He used this hardship to prepare me to gain strength and stand
To raise two children that he blessed me with, single handed
No this is not the way I would have planned it
It did not feel good but now I do understand it

When I was a teenager I never went out
Taking care of my family was all my life was about
For some reason I felt I had to fill daddy's vacant slot
And sometimes lies, hate and bitterness is the thanks I got

Oh but my God had a much greater plan
He gave me faith and love and now I can stand
Look in the face of every boy, girl, woman and man
And tell the world
That God ordered my steps and he held my hand
When I was lost I didn't find him but he found me
I will always Love my God and stay on my bending knees

Because I know that before I could even see, I realize now that my God first saw me
He doesn't supply just some you see, but he supplies every one of my needs
Words cannot express what God means to me
I will always give thanks, worship, pray, and praise my Jesus
Thank God from heaven above
He took care of me when I was

MUCH TOO YOUNG

At this age I think it's impossible
But she says we are very responsible
I know it seems like the right thing to do
But really doesn't it seem odd to you

We both are kind of young it would be good if we wait
But then again you already said you are too late
I hope you think long and hard about this creation
Because we are really in a hostile situation

We are really not ready to have this seed
Honey we don't know what this baby needs
We are making a big mistake I do believe
I am a little scared for we have already conceived

So to take the child's life is not an option for me
I will have to tough it out, and find a way please
I am so scared and I am so confused
I really don't know what in the world to do

I don't even know if I can go on in school
My classmates, shun me they are so cruel
Sometimes they can be extremely rude
So now I will have to make some kind of move

We are too young to know which way to go
I have never in my life felt so low
So my next thing is to go down on our knees
Cry out to God and ask him to help us please
Teenage pregnancy is no fun
I am unprepared, scared and much too young

Hold my head up right or wrong
Now that it is done I must live on
Even though I am much too young

TODAY

Today I arose of no strength of my own
I was extremely grateful, I wasn't alone
God breathed on me very gently
His love was felt deep inside of me

Today the Holy Spirit will be my guide
For Gods love deeply abides
Within my mind body and soul
I thank my God for today he's in control

Today will never come my way again
So I am going to try and make the best of it
For tomorrow will take care of itself
So today I will rely on Gods help

Today he helped me to remain calm
Today he awaken me it was not my alarm
So in my heart I will keep a song
Nothing for me today will go wrong

Today I will feel and sing my song
Jesus loves me all the day long
He loves me when I am right
And he even loves me when I am wrong

Today I am a little closer to heaven
Today I will be happy and just count my blessings
Today today today What more can I say
I thank My God today and everyday
As I kneel down to him and pray
I thank my God just for Today

IN LOVING MEMORY OF MY DADDY

My Love I am really very grateful
For the times we had to share
I thank the Lord for the many times
He has shown me just how much he cares

Twenty seven years ago, man had given you up
Oh how God, let me see, that you were not living on luck
Our heavenly father used you to allow me to see
Just how powerful and loving, Jesus Christ could really be

I've seen you so many times approaching deaths door
Just when you seemed to be giving up, God raised you up once more
Your life has truly been a living testimony
God used you miraculously so many times and you didn't even know it

Through your pain and suffering in this earthly tabernacle
I've come to know a lot about the true and living savior
I cherish the memories of Gods powerful hand
As he performed these miracles in your life I do understand
That he didn't have to let me see, he could have chosen any man

So daddy your life have allowed me to actually see
What some of God true believers, will only ever dream
Yes there are some who will never see, naturally all the mighty acts
of God
That I saw
I am thoroughly convinced that my Lord God Almighty only sees
the heart
God proved that to me by how he just kept on bringing you back
While the devil kept rapidly launching his vicious death attacks

Many thought and have even said; Oh he is no good
There is not a thought or a word that can over ride the Lord
God proved himself by the Holy Spirit and all the lives
He has used you to bless
(During your many visits in unc hospital)
That what others considered nothing and possibly mess
God truly let me know, that he considered you the best

I know your journey may have seemed long and extremely hard
So all of those times when folks, thought they knew you, but didn't understand
God has shown me, its Okay (Thaddeus) a disciple
You are really my chosen man

So daddy I may think of you sometimes and allow a tear to drop
In the midst I'll think of Gods goodness then the tears will soon stop
So daddy your oldest daughter Phyllis a very humbled child
Can only be grateful to God for the time I spent with you
I must pray, give God thanks and keep on smiling too

I will always cherish your life that God has shared
I will always give him praise for the many times your life he spared
It's really not very easy to have to let you go,
Because I love you daddy, but I know God loves you most
Now I must release you as God has his way
I will not say good-bye but I will simply say
Sleep on; sleep on my love sleep on
Your living has not been in vain

Loving Memory
January 8, 1998

RESPECT

Respect goes a long long ways
I don't care what nobody says
Respect is also a double duo
Notice if you give respect it comes back to you

I know there may be times that people are cruel
But that should not take away the respect in you
No matter how ugly one may be
You must say to yourself, you won't take away my dignity

The young must respect the old so
The old must respect the young too you know
Respect is priceless, however it could cost
No respect for yourself and others
You could find yourself lost
Respecting one another really shouldn't be hard
When we realize if we can't respect each other
Then how can you respect God

It is just not something we put aside
Lack of respect is something that you cannot hide
It goes with you wherever you go
Respect is a primary, part of the human growth

Love and Respect goes hand in hand
Why because it is in Gods plan
That we love and respect every woman and man
This is something he really wants us to clearly understand

There is no end to love and respect
It should always be operating in your mental shelf

Never forget to show respect for yourself
Then it will not be hard to respect every one else

SOMETHING IS WRONG

We have more people concerned about a flag on a pole
Than we have people concerned about their Souls
There was not this much controversy when Jesus was hung
Jesus our Lord and Savior was hung on a pole
Not just for me but for everyone's soul

Yes Jesus was hung on a pole and he was dying
Instead of crying for his life, they said oh crucify him
Little did they know, that he had the power to come down
But he wanted his father to keep smiling and not frown
He knew his life was to be given in exchange for a crown

The crown he won was for my life and yours
Something is wrong, when humans make more noise
About a flag hanging on a pole called con fed e rate
Than for a man called Jesus whose life was full of righteousness

Jesus is holy and full of love and righteousness
He truly died so that you and I could be blessed
We take his blessings and throw them all away
Instead of appreciating his love we boast and spread hate

Hang a hate flag high up on a pole, boldly wanting everyone to know
That your little flag stands for envy and hate, uh isn't that cold
Something is wrong with the heart of man, and Jesus knows
That's why he died for all lost souls
That's really truly why Jesus suffered so long
Because he knew in the heart of mankind, that something is wrong

Something is wrong, Yes Something is wrong
We spend more time of destruction tearing up homes

Than we spend letting God the father take control
We need to take Jesus off the pole
He died for mines and your very own soul

It is quite obvious that some of us still have him there
That's why there is too much hate and not enough care
Oh yes there is too much hate everywhere
Jesus is on the pole, he is not in your heart
Something is wrong people; take him down, and let's make a new start
Please take Jesus off the cross and place him in your heart

Let's hang a flag of Love and let it Fly Fly Fly
Jesus hung there for Love, he didn't have to die
We can move all the other flags and let's stop complaining
Let the Flag of Love Fly High, in Jesus Name

SMILES

Smiles can mean so many things to so many people
Smiles can even be a form of inner healing
Smiles can be contagious to some
Then oops it can be offensive to one

Isn't it funny how sometimes your smile comes back to you
Then there are other times you are left feeling or wondering what did
I do
A smile is only happy if it is happy to you
It can be and insult to another and even make them feel blue
Sounds strange but believe me it's true

Whatever the case whatever you do
Please don't ever let anyone take your smile from you
After all it is what you want it to be
Whether it makes you sad or very happy

Smiles smiles they express kindness sometimes
Smiles can bring someone a piece of mind
Never hold back on your precious little smile
It could actually be well worth your time

I remember a co-worker of mine
Made a really big deal about my simple little smile
She said my smile kept her from committing suicide
I thought oh my God, tears of joy I began to cry
When I realized a life was really saved, through my giving a smile

So with that thought in mind, no matter what you do
I mean I don't care what life takes you through
Don't ever let anyone take your smile from you

You may feel sad sometimes and perhaps even blue
But please don't let anyone take your smile from you

A smile is such a priceless thing to give
Who knows your smile just may help another one live
So go ahead give a smile people whatever you do
It will make the world a better place for me and for you

SMILE

THE DEATH IN THE WIND

Life has many amazing elements
But never anything so amazing as the wind
I often think to myself how calm it feels
Than again it can be forceful and take one for a spin

The wind is something that I cannot see
But yet I can feel it, oh yes feel it all over me
Not only is it all over me
It even breathes internally
For every living creature and human being

I have seen human beings who act so strong and bad
I look, I see, and sometimes feel truly sad
Because some men seems to have no common sense
I recognize that there is a powerful strength in the elements

A man can decide how he will spend his day
But what happens during the day only God can say
So he can let the wind blow very very soft
And then again he can let it tear the whole roof off

So I wonder why must people live as if they are in control
They hurt, and hate, be cruel and harm innocent souls
Some think being bad and strong is really what's happening
When God can let death actually be in the wind

So somebody tell me who has the power to stop the wind
Could it be James West, Super Man or maybe you my friend
I wish someone could help me understand, man
That is why the cruelty and power struggles should end
When you realize, that not any human strength can compare to

To the power of God and what he can do
So the violence, hatred, and fighting should all end
All God has to do is just blow, and there could be death in the wind

Breathe love peace and unity

PAIN FREE

My Lord and Savior died just for you and me
He endured much suffering; his life was not pain free
That is the way it had to be strategically
Some say salvation is free, but I say it was very costly
It cost a man his life so that you and I could be free

I know that not one of us paid this precious price
God sent his son who willingly gave his life
As a ransom for all, it was a great sacrifice
He lived in obedience, as he paid with his life

Now one thing that I am beginning to see
And that is because Jesus stood faithful and died for me
I have both a choice and a chance to become pain free
This earth is just a place to work on perfection you see
Cause where Jesus is, Is where I'm going to be
He died for me to have a home eternally

Because Adam and Eve did commit sin
I was born with pain from deep within
I had no real choice in the matter
In the Garden of Eve, it was my life the snake was after

When he began to glimpse at Adam and talk with Eve
The devil knew his lies Eve would believe
For that reason alone there is pain within
Disobedience allowed sin to step in

It started in the Garden of Eden, from the very beginning
When deception and disobedience truly came alive
That is when pain and trouble arrived

Not just for him her or you and me
But for every living human being

Oh you thought pain hit when you couldn't pay the bills
Or perhaps when doctor told you to take those pills
Or just maybe when lies and dishonesty you began to feel
But let me tell you what my God revealed

Honey pain came about where sin lived
It happened when flesh disobeyed Gods will
This is a promise that has been fulfilled
That is why God Sent Jesus to carry out his will
Jesus suffered and died so willingly
So that you and I can become pain free
So before you tell someone salvation is free
Remember to tell them Jesus paid for me

Jesus came for strictly business and not a flesh party
He wants our mind, soul and body
His desire for me is to become pain free
He wants me to live eternally
That's why he truly died for me

Oh yes I can even financially
Through the spirit of Christ, become pain free
All because Jesus Christ died for me
I can also be healed emotionally
All because Jesus Christ died for me
I realize now it is totally left up to me
Whether or not I choose to be free
Financially, physically, and emotionally
I can have it all if I live spiritually
Because Jesus took all the hurt and pain for me
It is truly my choice to become pain free

NOW WHAT

I have given my life to Christ now what
My life of sin I have now given up
You said that Gods word is really true
But I can't see a God in you

I hear his word it says to love my neighbor as myself
It appears that you have stored love on the shelf
I don't see love in your actions although I hear what you say
Your love must be deep in your heart it is not on display

So I am suppose to Love you I understand
But you don't seem to be obeying Gods command
I am trying to hold on to Gods unchanging hand
I am struggling trying to love my fellow man

You are back biting and so sometimes I bite back
I never knew Christians could be like that
I had my share of that when I was in the world
Smoking them blunts and shooting them curves

Yes I lied; I played games and broke all of Gods rules
Until one day I realized I was being a fool
I wanted to change my life and I gave it all up
My heart of stone is now a heart of love
I chose to stop all my sinning and that rough stuff
So Christians by your actions can you tell me
NOW WHAT

NO TEST NO TESTIMONY

Testimonies are told all the time
Life is full of test with no reason nor rhyme
What makes a man just lie down to sleep
And the next morning he can't even move his feet

Oh as if moving the feet was the real problem
I had a brain, filled with problems that couldn't even think on how to solve them
My body was attacked with a thing called an aneurism
I have nerves in my body and I couldn't even feel them
The doctor looked at my father and said
Sir by to tomorrow morning, your son will be dead

My father responded, If I was a betting man
I would bet you everything that I have
To prove to you that tomorrow, my son's life will still stand
Because daddy knew, my life was in Gods Hand

In fact he said to the doctor on the floor
You just don't know the man that I know
By Gods grace he will live his life and grow
I am very very sure, cause my Jesus tells me so

I use to think my job and cars and money was everything
Until God laid me down, and then raised me up again
While I was resting in the hands of my God
Before this thing happened, I thought I was living large

I thought I was on top of the world
I had a job, car, house, money and a crazy girl
I thought she was a wife and a very good friend

But when this storm hit me, she blew with the wind

Oh do I have a testimony
I can truly say Jesus will never leave me lonely
I got more Love and Peace than I've ever known
Not a day goes by and finds me mad or sad
Jesus Christ has healed me and I am truly glad

New Friends, he has supplied
God proves to me, on him I can rely
He gives me money, true friends, Love, Joy, and Peace
I thank God for my Test and my Testimony

Jesus Christ is the best you see
Everyone should pray and Trust God as he leads
Go ahead just relax, let God lead the way; people please
Cause without a test there is no testimony

NINE ELEVEN

When those planes struck the towers on nine eleven
Many people start praying to our father in heaven
But it only took a few short days
For people to change back to their mean old ways

Everyone seem more gentle and greetings with smiles
But you know what that only lasted for a little while
Tragedy has a way of bringing people to a halt
Then suddenly war begins, because someone's at fault

Instead of trusting God and continue on praying
Man decides to take matters into his own hands
So we deploy all of our soldier boys
Off to Iraq without giving them a choice

Many American families are feeling the pain
Because we have to go after Sudam Hussein
Oh yes we started to fight and go after this man
Instead of continuing to pray in Jesus name
We must capture him for he is the blame

The planes, the war, not any man is the problem
It is a thing called disobedience that could solve this
World of madness that keeps us a part
Don't look at the planes, but look in our hearts

If we continue to disobey our Fathers words
There will continue to be disasters like you never heard
So we must stop, look, and listen to God
Let's stop gambling with life as if it is a deck of cards
If you think living is really hard, you just try dying without the Lord

Nine eleven was just a wakeup call from heaven
Don't' fall asleep and turn away
Stay on your bending knees and pray
Not only for ourselves but for the whole nation
Instead of Nine Eleven being a tragedy, it could be your greatest blessing

Nine eleven
Reminds me to pray twenty four seven
Thank you, Jesus and Praise God in heaven

MY LITTLE BIT OF HOPE

We are born into this world but little do we know
About just which way this life will go
We are born into a thing called families without having any choice
Guess what life came about from Gods spoken voice

He decided to create a man and he created a woman
Then he ordered them to be fruitful and produce children
He has many rules that are already in place
He has rules for me you and the entire human race

This man called Adam an a woman named Eve
Had everything in the Garden that they would ever really need
But somehow Brother Adam along with Sister Eve
Changed the course of life that was planned for all humanity

They disobeyed the truth that God conveyed
Instead Eve paid attention to what the snake had to say
This is the beginning of why we have to struggle
Instead of obeying God they both was kicked out of the Garden

So now I have had a few struggles of my own
But somehow in the midst of the madness, I discovered I was never alone
When I was a teenager I wanted to commit suicide
Because I was trapped in a family where very little peace abided
I use to just go to my room and break down and cry
I would silently ask the question again and again why
I felt so much misery I truly wanted to die

So I started thinking of ways to end my young life
Would it be pills, drugs, or perhaps a gun or a knife?

Well to add more agony to all my hurt and my pain
I went to a party and was raped by a man

To add injury to insult, and a loss of hope
I became pregnant by a man I didn't know
I was scared and ashamed and felt extremely low
But that little child inside was my little bit of hope

I no longer had a choice to commit suicide
Because there was a little precious life growing inside
My mother just fussed and false accused me so
But little did my dear mother know
That little baby inside was my little bit of hope

So I kept my little baby and I loved her so
I began to gain strength and let being ashamed actually go
No longer ashamed of my teenage pregnancy you know
I thought I must let pain go, because surely everyone will reap what they sow
I was guided by God to just live and let the baby grow
Because actually deep inside of me was my little bit of hope

Some may hear this poem and say oh how sad
But believe me I am a sister that is truly glad
To say that God knows best for every child woman and man
He has proven to me that what the devil meant for bad you know
It is just a trap to let the devil, know that Jesus lives and he is still in control
And because of God I now stand boldly to say hold on to hope

LONELY BUT NOT ALONE, THIS TIME

Sometimes from the sunrise to the sunset
Loneliness shows me my happiness
This could be very confusing
Could my mind sometimes be just an illusion

My mind tells me I'm lonely and I cry
Oh could my mind be telling me a lie
It's hard to make sense of this cyclone
I am lonely at times but yet not alone

Somehow me, myself, and I
Breaths to know me deep down inside
While the outside boast in great pride
No I am not lonely, this I do hide

Who am I hiding from them or me
Yes one part of me cries help I am lonely
While another part screams, don't let them see
That you are lonely and alone, smile and just go on

Go on lying to yourself while , one part cries Holy and another
Part cries help
Holy! Holy! Holy! , Lord God My Savior
Help! Help! Help! Lord I don't know if I am able

I don't know if I am able to go on this way
I must stop this nonsense and let Jesus control my Day
This I pray as he began to lead the Way
I must stop loneliness and living a lie
Jesus is with me now, I am not alone this time

I no longer need to continue to try and hide
What I am truly feeling deep down inside
Yes loneliness is present but I'm not alone this time
Jesus in not only in me but he stands by my side

So look at me now , I have nothing to hide
Because now Jesus is living on the inside
No you don't see anyone standing by my side
I am not alone it is me and Jesus this time
I can truly say Jesus is mine
He paid the debt but I did the crime
Yet he continues to be by my side
I may appear lonely, but I am not alone this time

LAST NIGHT I SAW A MAN

Last night I saw a man who looked so bright and fair
I didn't mean too but I really couldn't help but stare
The look on his face was so full of grace and peace
This look of peace on his face could calm a raging sea

There were others sitting behind him in complete silence
He was looking ahead with much peace and he was smiling
I saw him shrug his shoulders very gently
He must to have been talking to God evidently

It was as if he was sitting before a judge
He was focusing straight ahead as he held his head up
Never even looking around to see who was in his presence
I thank he already knew, he was surround by students as he took instructions
Not so much for himself but for others to learn a lesson

The lesson I learned as I watched this man
Is to stay focused and pay close attention
To the instructions that's being given by the judge
This is one of the greatest lessons about life and love

He was so calm, so attentive and so full of peace
As I watched him I thought how can I thank him as I bowed to my knees
When you see him you can't do nothing but bow
You must ask the question, someone killed him. I really want to know how. How could anyone crucify my Jesus and yours?
For he is Lord and Savior of all living souls

AND GOD

The book of Genesis is filled with and God
Without his words creativity would be hard
You see without him there would only be night

And God saw the light it was good
Light only exist today because of his spoken word
And God called the light day
Now you and I can see our way

And God said let there be an firmament
He is strictly business what he said is what he meant
All he had to do was speak what he wanted
At his spoken word it now appears as he called it

And God said let there be waters under heaven
Be gathered together under into one place
Now we have people killing one another and claiming their space
Acting as if they created this world you know
It was God who said let the dry land appear and it was so

And God said let the earth bring forth grass
God is so full of power and righteousness
What he spoke from Genesis to Revelations
Is ours to see as a true realization
It is not just an infatuation
It is Gods true revelation

And God is still speaking today
Do you know there is life also in what you say?
The power of life and death is in our tongue
That's why we should always use God's spoken words

And God said man should not live by bread alone
But we should live by every word he has spoken
He also said he gave us life and gave it abundantly
And that's Gods eternal promise to both you and me
And God lives on

BUT GOD

When I think of where I have been in my life
I sometimes began to think of the trouble, the struggles and the strife
I often think of where I possibly could have been
If Jesus Christ had not been my precious friend

I could have been in a mental institution
Because my life has been one big ball of confusion
I am grateful for Jesus Christ being my friend
Because my life for a while just didn't make any sense
Although there are times when life is really hard
I am honored to be able to say BUT GOD

Yes I probably would have been destroyed or even dead
If not from the blows I've endured, then certainly from what they said
They said I was no good, and wouldn't amount to anything
But while they was talking, I was praying in Jesus Name
I had no time to waste or place the blame
Satan had a battle on his hand with me you see
It was not a fight physically
This battle is fought on bended knees

I found out that there is power in his name
And although I have my faults, Jesus loves me just the same
Some have actually looked me in my face and said
You know you really ought to be dead
These words to my ears was really harsh
But the spirit in my heart, shouted BUT GOD

But God sent his son from heaven you see
So that I could live, life abundantly
Yes he gave his life specifically for you and me

Not only to live abundantly, but so we could live eternally

But God has truly set me free
I will praise his name boldly, as he keeps preparing me
To depart from this temporary residence and go home you see
When I see him, I may pause for a moment and take a nice long glance
Then I will walk around heaven, and do my dance

I am going to praise him daily as the Angels does
I will praise him forever, for he has shown such great love
He came willingly from heaven above
The preparation of the gospel of peace, my feet have been shod
You see I could have been dead, but I stand today and say BUT GOD
Halleujah I can stand today and say
The devil tried to destroy me and take me away
But GOD- delivered me from the enemy
But God- shed blood saved me, now I believe
But God –touched my heart and awakened me
So that I could be all that he wants me to be

Yes the Devil tried to kill everything within me
But God- has truly set me free
Not just today or temporary
It is throughout eternity
Everything in this world changes, but Gods word remains the same
So there is no excuse for defeat, or anyone to blame
People and circumstances, may change or maybe even things
But God never changes, His love will always remain the same in
Jesus Name

So today I have no one to hate, I have no one to blame
I just have a God to glorify and a Savior to praise
I will just keep right on loving just the same
Praising him is a delight it is not very hard
I can only pray and give thanks and
SHOUT BUT GOD

LET GOD

I often hear the phrase let go and let God
Saying words is easy, but for some living them is hard
When it comes to letting God, I have something to say
If you're going to let God, have his way
Then you must first began to pray

I've tried too many times to move on my own
And it seem like every way I turned was wrong
Until one day I stopped and stood still you know
I just dropped to my knees, in my living room floor

I had enough of doing things my way
So I let go of my ways and began to pray
I really did not know exactly what to say
But I could not go on another day
So I sincerely ask God to lead the way
My life has never never been the same
Jesus heard my cry and he made a change

It was not until I let go sincerely
That my God would allow me to see
That evil forces was all around me
The devil had the lock, but I had given him the key

I gave him the key when I refused to believe
That God sent his son Jesus to die just for me
So I trusted boyfriends, girlfriends, and even family too
For a long time, I really didn't think Gods word was true

It was not until these folk hurt me so, until I didn't know what to do
I felt like I couldn't even see how to make it through

All of the pain, the hurt and the disappointment to
Although it was really truly hard
I decided, I've tried everything else why not try God

After holding on to pains that hurt me so
I finally decided, I must let go
Let go of how they make me feel
In exchange to do my Gods will

Let go of how they told me lies
In exchange for a higher prize
Let go of believing in what they said
To trust God, and practice every word he said
Let Go of my doubt and disbelief
Even though trusting God was new to me
Although this faith walk was not very easy
I decided to be patient with them and me
I am not in a race you see
I am simply seeking Gods peace
After all he did die just to set me free
And the ultimately thing we need is peace

Now I can tell the world today
That to let go of your worldly ways
You will absolutely have to pray
Not one but each and every day
Let God's spirit lead you every step of the way
Let God forever keep you in his grace
So that one-day we will see him face to face

IF GOD

If God was not self existent
There would be no life; no nothing would be living
If God is not our heavenly creator
Then please tell me people who are your maker

I've seen a lot of creations that was made by man
But I never seen life, being made by hands
Wonder what makes a human heart beat
I don't think you can truly explain it

If God created us in his image
We should at least acknowledge him for the life that we are living
Most of all simply for the life he has given
If God sent his only son to suffer for us as he went
Then certainly the least we can do is simply repent

If God forgave all those that done him wrong
I am sure all of us, should be at his throne
Asking him forgiveness, for what we have done
Giving him thanks for not leaving us all alone

If God dealt with us according to our ways
We probably wouldn't even have a chance to pray
If God could love us enough to give his son
Then certainly we should show him more love and concern
We should set our affections on things above
Live a life that's pleasing to God and filled with his love
Why because God really loves us inspite of

If God can love us inspite of
Then we should thank him for such great love

In everything we say and do
Because let's face it, this is a thought that's true
Without God there would be no me or you
It's scary to think about what would happen you see
If God for just one second decides to stop loving you and me

WHEN GOD

When God comes into your life
It's like and eraser and sometimes a knife
He wipes away many pains and tears
He even cuts away misery and fears

When God moves in your heart and calls your name
Your whole entire life began to change
You will never ever be the same
In fact your appetite began to change
The things you were proud of now make you a shame
You no longer state to the claim to fame
For you realize the worlds way was just a game
But Jesus Christ is the real thing

When God removes things from our life
He does not delight in causing you strife
God does not remove one thing without giving
You a greater reward, which is his precious Holy Spirit

When God gives you his Holy Spirit
He empowers you to live a life that is fulfilling
Yes Gods Holy Spirit enables us to live
Not by one but by every command that he gives

When God is present in our lives
The Holy Spirit is like x-ray eyes
It sees the things, the natural eye can't see
The Holy Spirit is a superb guide for both you and me

IF EYES COULD TALK

If your eyes could talk
Tell me what they would say
As you greet your sister and brothers each day
Would they lift someone's spirit along the way?

Would your eyes be as a sharp knife blade?
Cutting them in every which way
Oh if your eyes could talk my brother what would they say?
Oh sister tell me what message do your eyes convey

Well eyes say much more than they see
Eyes tell the truth of how you feel about me
A smile on your lips makes me ask the question why
Do your eyes spell hate, but yet your lips are still smiling

I see much more than your lips are saying
Look in your soul, what are your eyes portraying
Do your eyes express the image of God?
Cause if so, then I should see Love

Oh taste and See that the lord is good
What do I see when I look at you
Hush don't move your lips boo
I will just let your eyes tell me the truth

No need to change your composer now
Cause God sees the heart anyhow
Eyes reveal more than you thought
Tell me what you would say if your eyes could talk

LIFE IS YOURS TO EXPLORE

Life is a journey that everyone must travel
There are dreams and visions that we seek after
As we sometimes travel down life's road
There are times when we feel that it is a heavy load

I'm sure there are moments it seems; there are not enough hours in the day
Long night's short days, and you're just in maize
But somehow you still seem to find your way
These are the times when you really learn to pray

The journey of life is not always smooth
But even in the midst of the roughness, you believed in you
You trusted God, yourself and you kept right on moving
As you trusted God to never leave you alone as he has proven

Special friends and even enemies may come and they will go
But even they are a part of your growth
So while you are traveling down life's lane you see
Some experiences are just simply meant to be
You know what? a tree cannot stand without a root honey

Oh yes roots run deep and they provide much stability
So people come and go you see
Guess what? even your enemies
Helps to push you to your destiny
Sometimes that's what it takes to strengthen thee
Without a deep root of determination honey please
There is no way you could possibly
Stand tall and be all that you desire to be
And of course prayer and faith which is the key

Your education is another key that unlocks a door
This journey of life is yours to explore
Oh what a blessing it is for the accomplishments you have made
Today is only the beginning of a road you and God have paved
You know another thing, I would like to say
I believe that you have what it takes to climb heavens stairway

Haven't you heard the old saying, The Sky is the limit
I believe you are on your way, if you just keep God in it
You're beautiful, you're bright and you have a loving heart
I encourage you today as you receive your degree and make a new start
Darling just keep praying and always trust God

For I know it is God who gives you the ability
To become all, and <u>then some</u> that you desire to be
If ever in doubt just go down on bended knees
For it is by Gods grace that you have achieved
And excelled in your life academically
I thank God for your intellectuality
And I'm sure you do too, because you have expressed that to me
Prayer is the vehicle and faith is the key

Remember life is truly yours to explore
You just keep running through those open doors
You are walking strong and taking all of the right steps
I Praise God for you, for you have truly been blessed
To be able to stand with some of the best
One of whom can stand tall with all the rest
For I realize the journey of life is a real true test

Well no matter how high the rest may soar
You too can enter through that open door
Oh yes the journey of life is yours to explore
last but not least I would like to say
As I close this poem and continue to pray

Every word I have spoken I certainly meant it
I Love you honey and I believe the Sky is your limit

Keep Soaring and Fly High
With Gods help you can reach the stars

DO WHAT YOU LIKE

In this world we have no boundaries
Jesus Christ is the creator and the founder
I'm told in the word that this world was void
Light came about the from his spoken word

God just opened his mouth and said let there be
What ever he spoke is what we now see
Without his words there would be no you or me
He even sent his son to set us free

Do what you like was made possible by Jesus
He live died and suffered just to free us
Oh but let me tell you he did not stop there
He was buried and got up with all power in his hands
Just to show us how much he really cares

He gave us choices, oh yes we can choose
To do anything our little heart wants to do
Choose ye this day whom you will serve
Says my friend Joshua, in Gods holy word

It is such a blessing that he didn't make us all robots
We can choose to abide in his word or we can choose disobey God
He said there would be battles that we don't even have to fight
Cause Jesus has paid a price for you to do what you like
No matter if it is wrong or right

So whether you choose to obey him or not
Is really not my problem that is between you and your God
It is not my job to judge you, hate you, argue or even fight
Cause only you have to answer to God, so do what you like

A MAN IS NEVER A FAILURE UNTIL

A man is never a failure until he blames someone else
If you don't receive your sisters or your brothers help
Then I strongly suggest, you to just help yourself
Never think that if they fail you then it won't get done
You must do it; yes you You are the only one

Life is a race that must be won
You may never become a star or run a marathon
But you must rely on you to get the job the done
Do what no one else will,(<u>for you</u>) cause you are the only one

Who's the blame for your lack of fame?
Who's the blame for your low self-esteem?
Whatever happened that was meant to kill you
God intended it all, simply to build you, who?

You yes you and only you, they are not the blame
You fail to believe in yourself and in Jesus Name
Success is failure turned inside out
So what is all the finger pointing and blaming all about?

I know sometimes life makes you want to Holler
Connecting with folk sometimes you say why even bother
Sometimes confused about what life is really all about
Look for other avenues, and a quick way out
I'll add my little two cents worth today
I'll say a man is not a failure until he refuses to pray
Again I'll say I know sometimes life makes you want to Holler
Let me take you just a little bit further
Just one more little tip of info for you
Just try this when you don't know what to do

If you really looking for a way out
Start with Repentance, Prayer, and Praise and give God a Shout

HOLLA

CAUSE IT'S BOTHERING ME

I really understand very clearly
To lend a hand is the way life should be
Although there are times when life is filled with simplicity
I must admit there are times when some things just bother's me

Let me try to explain this thing explicitly
A situation I'm dealing with that's bothering me
You see I met a person in college while earning my degree
One of whom, became a friend to me

Friends are held dear to your heart
They are considered to be someone you respect
With this respect we have a tendency
Try to help in any way you can you see

My friend needed a place to stay
So she came to me one troubled day
Wanted to live with me at my place
I said okay for two months to stay, since I had the space

Well now times is moving on
Two months has come and gone
This person is still living in my home
Not making any plans to be on her own

Now I must put it quite simply
I want them to go because it's bothering me
There are other friends who will not even come to visit me
Because this person is still living there, and it's bothering me

I am trying to be patient and as nice as can be

But my God this thing is bothering me
My girlfriend says she will handle it respectfully
But My God this situation is really bothering me

I chatted with a lady about this concern you see
She suggested very humorously, Honey why don't you call the police
Put her clothes on the front porch, very nicely
Cause my God, this thing is really bothering me
I have got to do something very quickly
Because this thing is truly bothering me

Not paying one bill as they steadily increase
At this point I don't even want any money
I just simply want them gone you see
Cause this thing is really really bothering me

CAUSE THEY ARE USING ME

I found out something that carries me through
It is very hard for people to use you, when God is using you
It is nothing so great that anyone can do
It is just simply who God decides to choose

I use to be so hurt, by what folk say and do
No matter how nice I was and how sincere or true
I would always end up feeling like I had been used
Neglected rejected and abused
Not to mention being left feeling like a fool
Wow sometimes people can be so cruel

One-day a quiet still voice spoke so soft and cool
It said honey don't take it personal you are just the tool
I decided you were the one I wanted to use
Much like Abraham he was simply the man God wanted to choose
So no need to scream and make a lot of noise
Just please remember you are simply God's choice

Don't worry go ahead and let them think you are defeated
It's not you lending time, love, and talent you see
I gave you life and gave it to you more abundantly
Cause they was not using you, it was actually me

Greater is he that is in me than he that is in the world
The Lord says I am he the one that breathe my spirit in you girl
So I took you places you didn't even want to go
But the me inside of you just loved me so
So you gracefully allowed me to run the show
I took you to some places in life, you didn't even know
It has been a very effective part of your spiritual growth

The body, soul and mind was dragging your behind
You went to assist them with lots of love joy and a smile
When you could have been checking your own pulse and somewhere crying
Or pleasing satan by perhaps even spiritually dying
About all of the things life have thrusted upon you
But you love me so much that your heart refused too

Now all you need to do my darling is press on the upward way
I'll take care of them; I have something to say
You just keep right on pressing, praising, and always pray
They must watch how they treat kindness and serenity
Cause honey they were not using you, they were actually using me
No it was not one person but it was really three, because I am the trinity

So go ahead keep smiling as you bend your knees
Whatever you do, just keep praising me please
I am your God and I will supply not some but all of your needs
Just keep right on living and loving you see
Cause they was not using you it was actually me

FEELINGS

I have a calling upon my life
I don't know what it will turn out to be
I do know God has something important for me to do
Something that will make a difference to many

I have these feelings that I don't understand
It's like I need to help everyone I can
I try to say and do those things
That will aid them in their everyday lives

It concerns me to see so many people looking for
The thing or things that will make their life complete
So I listen to all they have to say
Then I try to let God speak through me

Sometimes it's hard to keep my personal feelings
From spilling over into what God tells me to say
So I stop and think what his wishes are about it
Then let his voice lead me the right way

My ears hear more than the words they say
I can sense what is written between the lines
The things they don't say mean so much more
Than what's spoken in effort to disguise
What is truly the reason for their unhappiness
Kept from view, from most of mankind
In doing so they sometimes hide from themselves
The things that will free them from their own mind

I've been through a lot in my short lifetime
Ups and downs, troubles and strife have not pass me by

So I can relate to the problems they encounter
I try to aid them in making up their mind
Focus ahead and leave the past behind

I feel I am blessed with a sense of duty
To help all those who seek the truth
To share what God has given to me
And aid in someone's struggles/success in life

God has given me a heart of love and concern
Especially for those who seem unable to receive
Fulfillment from the things of this world
That promises to give pleasure and relief

I care about people no matter who or what they are
I try to look beyond, and beneath the façade
And see and feel what's hidden underneath
What's lying there. dormant, yearning to be free

A face they feel they need to portray
For what ever reasons they convince themselves
Should be shown as who and what they are
At times it's really the only way you can survive

But, lying beneath that outer surface
Is a vulnerable person, susceptible to pain
Afraid it may be used against them
And much of the time , that IS the case

So they keep up this face of deception
Hoping no one will uncover the real "self"
Secure, behind the shield that protects them
From people's eyes that can hurt and destroy

Destroy the fragile being lying there, watching
The people of this world that come to tear down
Anyone that shows weakness in any way

Or appears to the world to be easily persuaded

So, I listen, closely, hearing unspoken words
Feelings the anguish, seeing the real pain
Trying to separate myself from my feelings
Hoping to help someone along the way
Can you Feel the Feelings

GODS ANGEL CAME UPON ME

Life has a funny way of leading you
To places and things you did not choose
Sometimes pain can take you to the doctor's office
You don't know what happened and what really caused this
And so here you sit in a place you did not choose
Trying to explain what happen to you
Sometimes leaving even the doctor confused
Can't really get a clear view of what you are going through

So you sit with this person as he or she listens to you
Then they start to examine you too
Trying to bring relief and comfort you see
But the real pain is lying dormant, deep within me

Yes my bodily pains are real and truly hurts physically
But not nearly as bad as the pain deep within me
So I hurt both physically and emotionally
So my pain is being treated physically
But there is a deep pain that no one can see
It hurts my heart internally
Creates deep pain emotionally
Then my pain escalates physically
It took me quite some time to began to see
That one of Gods Angels had came upon me
The prescription and therapy all helped you see
But even more importantly
He took the time to listen to me
Not only with his ears but with his heart completely

For the first time in my life
I did not even realize

How I had been arrested internally, by some pretty bad things
That was locked inside causing me double pain

So as I opened my mouth to speak
He listened to me very patiently
That alone was medicine for me
I didn't realize just how much I'd been set free
From that internal pain that was killing me
Some may call him a mere man, therapist or a great physician
I see with my heart, my soul and my spirit
He is much more than a mere man, or anything else you see
One of Gods Angels Came upon Me
Perhaps some day I can earn my wings
And hopefully we will meet again
If not here on earth perhaps in the wind
As the spirit leads us to our end
I will always remember you and your ability
To keep my pain calm and at ease
Hope you don't forget about me

It is my prayer that God will keep using you
And enable you to keep doing what you do
I am grateful that I had the opportunity
To say that One of Gods Angels Came Upon Me

FORGIVEN

I use to be so careless in the life I was living
Not realizing that I had already been truly forgiven
Unworthy, shame and guilt was what I was feeling
The thought of letting go of the guilt was not too appealing

Actually I really didn't know how to let go
Because living a life of sin is not to pretty you know
So I just let blind friends, and my twisted thoughts run the show
Until one day I reached a point that I could not take any more

Going to church wasn't to mundane, I showed up every Sunday
I tried going to the altar kneeling to pray
But as I got up turned and walked away
The guilt shame and sorrow all seemed to stay
But I just kept going to church anyway

I found out where the problem lived
I had not learn how to forgive
Not only others but myself as well
God had freed me, but I was still under my spell

A spell of fear, doubt and unbelief
Didn't realize Jesus truly lived and died just to set me free
He didn't hold guilt over me
It was my blinded eyes that could not see
I found it so hard to truly believe
But oh what a great change came over me
When I finally got rid of my unbelief

I learned and believed that this man named Jesus
Would do anything if I just truly believe him

So I believe that Jesus Christ was forsaken you see
To enable us to forgive others and especially me

Now I no longer live in guilt and shame
I am free in Jesus Name
No longer placing the blame for how I am living
My God assures me that I have been forgiven

But I am not so ignorant; I know it's not a one time deal
I must keep repenting and asking for forgiveness as long as I live
I am grateful to God, for this peace I am feeling
No man can give this except by the spirit
I truly thank God for his holy spirit
That assures me, that I have been forgiven

I AM

I am the queen/king of the universe
Because God created man from the dust of the earth
He then put man into a deep sleep
And from his rib he created you and me

I am the breath that my God breathes
When he blew breath into brother Adam and sister Eve
He didn't stop there it was for you and for me
That's why I am so special you see
Because the breath I now breathe is Gods honey
And if that's not special then you tell me what is

I am created to be productive and free
I am created to celebrate the life of savior named Jesus
I am not to be treated without respect and dignity
I am a precious jewel, filled with peculiarity
I am everything that God says I can be

I am a lady/man of royal priesthood, and the temple of God
He made my body to worship him, and he fills my heart
With truth, guidance, direction and perfection
I am filled with Gods Love and his Affection

I am not to allow my body to be used and abused
I will strive to be wise and become no one's fool
So teenage pregnancy will not interfere with my schooling
Not just academically and most definitely not spiritually
I am going to embrace every little single tool
To become all God created me to be and not break his rules

I am the wisdom that my forefathers shared

I am the fruit of a savior who cared
I am not restricted to whom I receive love
Because after all, real love only comes from above
To those who will let love penetrate the heart
So God can began to grow his little special garden

I am the lesson that's taught to me by the young and the old
I am the blessing that is yet to be known
I am the branch that continues to be nurtured
I am the fulfillment of God's Divine purpose
My Destiny will happen in God's time and not a moment early

I AM GODS CHILD

I AM NOT HERE FOR ME

Sorry to say I am not here for me
I am not even here for you
I was created by God
To do what he tells me too
And he decides if my life includes you

Even when you treat me bad and hurt me so
I will not even physically try to fight you know
When God takes control, I won't even say I told you so
I will just let the Holy Spirit run this show
Cause God is the deliverer of my soul

Although I am not here for you
I just may be the vessel he is using
To point you to a street called straight
I am just behind the wheel but God leads my way

So don't take it personal when we reach your stop
If you have a problem with me then you must first see God
I learn more and more, this life of mine is not a buddy deal
Jesus purpose for me was strictly business
In fact in his word he actually says this
I must be about my fathers business
So I have a calling and a purpose to fulfill
Not by my power but by my Gods will

Really I mean really I am not here for you
I was truly created to do what God tells me too
I may start in one direction and he says no
So I quickly come to a halt and wait for him to say go

Although at times it appears he is a little slow
But he knows when and where I must go
I am convinced that if he doesn't tell me, then know one else knows
I am his handy work so he runs the show

His ways are just so much higher and different from mine
When I want to hold on tight just like twisted twine
Gods says let go, I will handle this and they will be fine
Even if they huff and puff and don't understand
God says trust me , let go now of that hand
For I have all power in my hand, and I am the man
And you were created to fulfill my plan
Please understand

I AM STILL HERE

Just like the spirit of the heavenly dove
I am still sitting on my throne above
I sent my son Jesus who was filled with love
He came down in flesh, but that wasn't enough
He suffered and died and then he got up

He rose with all power in his hand
Went back with his father please understand
His spirit was sent to every child, woman and man
His great love for his fellowman
Will empower everyone to stand

He looks down from heaven and watches over us
He sees all the friction, and he hears all of the fuss
The word says his eyes are in every place
He sees and hears every word we say

Sometimes we feel that he is not near
But please believe me God is still here
He is not deaf he hears really clear
And when you least expect him, he will appear

He warns us constantly to watch as well as pray
He never sleeps nor slumbers; he watches both night and day
So if you think you can hide your sin my dear

Gods Holy Spirit has a keen listening ear

He is not like man, who seeks to destroy
He watches over you so he can give you joy
He protects you from dangers seen and unseen
He has no respecter of person he loves every human being
You must believe that he knows all about you
Before you even thought it he knew what you would do

Jesus came willingly and suffered persecution and much abuse
So that you and I wouldn't have to
But not by force, only if we choose too
He didn't leave us without a way out
His words says I am the way the truth and the life
So there is no where to hide, be it far or near
Be still and listen Gods Holy Spirit says I am still here

WHAT'S IMPORTANT TO YOU

I was blessed to attend North Carolina Central University
To hear not one doctor but there was three
They were three black brothers who are very successful
They came to share words of wisdom to every listener
They each had some very powerful words to say as a matter of fact
That's why they called themselves the pact
They grew up in the tough streets of gangs and drugs
But they chose not to become professional thugs
In spite of all the many obstacles they had to face
They never stop believing in themselves no matter what anyone had to say
They studied hard and they kept the faith

They made a pact one day to become successful no matter what it takes
They looked around in their class room one day
Decided some may not make it but we must stay
I did hear one mention that he had to pray

The one doctor talked about how he loved being cool
But realized nothings more important than school
Although being cool was not completely omitted
He decided that if he really wanted to be cool, then he must get down with this
What is this one might ask
It is getting your mind focused and getting to class
What's important to you is what Dr. Jenkins said
It's not cool to have no knowledge in that head

Some may say girls or boys is my main focus
With no means of survival some may not even know you

Girls will come Guys will go
What's important to you, is a simple question so

What are you thinking my sister my brother
Only you can answer that question like no other
It was important for these brothers to achieve their goals
So they got their priorities in line and the rest was on hold
Maybe not completely because they did enjoy college life
They would get their studying done first, even if it took all night
I heard them say very distinctively
Getting an A was not just important to me
It was equally important for all three
So if one did well he didn't look down on the other
He simply shared his time and knowledge with his brother

What's important to you?
Everyone has to choose
What they want to become
When it's all said and done

These are some of the most powerful words anyone could ever ask
I keep hearing it ringing in my ears from one doctor in the pact
It doesn't matter what others think or even do
What really matters in life is what's important to you

WHO IS YOUR FATHER

I must be about my fathers business
This is the message Jesus was living
Yes Jesus was much more than some words spoken
Jesus was a living demonstration and not just a token

Oh but when we speak of the word our father from heaven
There is another father, who is called the devil
I read in the word that he is the father of lies
He is a liar, deceiver and a master of disguise

This is a serious thing for one to consider
Satan is the father of lies, but God himself is a strong deliverer
Whose child are you, everyone must ask themselves
Are you Gods child or are you a child of the devil

Hold on wait a minute don't answer me
Jesus has x-ray vision you see
He knew us right from the very start
We only see the flesh, God sees the heart

There are too many people today having issues with daddy
So they just ignore their father which is still in heaven
We poison our purpose and miss our blessings baby
Because we are too busy, making excuses and proudly blaming daddy

If you will face the real truth, trust God and his word obey
Confess with your mouth and let God lead the way
Listen, Listen please Listen hear what I say
God is your father and your daddy is not the blame
Although he may have caused you a little bit of pain
Jesus Christ is your healer and he is always the same

He loves you dearly and he knows your name
He died to save you and he never ever changes

So your daddy was just the tool that your Father has chose
To plant, and produce a seed that he needed to grow
Jesus is the one who will make you whole
So all your biological daddy did was to plant the seed
God is still alive wanting to supply your every need

So look up and rejoice, you are part of a business deal
God made a promise that he will fulfill
So why are you allowing your actions to prove
That the devil is a liar and a deceiver too

You looking for a daddy, when you already have a father
Instead of reading your bible you say why bother
God is a business man you must believe
If you want to know him, try bending your knees
He loves you and he really really cares
He's waiting to answer your every little prayer

The devil is a liar and was kicked out of heaven
He tries to stop not one but all of your blessings
It's the devil that places those thoughts of why bother
He don't want you to know that God is truly your father

God is your father and God is light and love
He was sent to die for our sins, from heaven above
Above him there is no other
He is the best and the greatest lover
He is even one of the greatest nurturer's
So instead of you saying why even bother
Let your actions began to show who truly is your father

MORE THAN I WANT TO SEE

You have shown me more than I want to see
I don't want to know you physically
Don't even want to know you sexually
I would rather get to know you spiritually

When it comes to being intimately
It will only happen the way God intended it you see
My Lord and savior is enough for me
Jesus Christ is more than able to satisfy my needs
And so I will just trust him whole heartily

If your only strength is in the bed
Then I don't want to hear a word you said
Without Gods Love, Sex could soon be dead
Our relationship will end up being a real true dread

Dread the day we ever even met
Because there was no real love, it was only flesh
Flesh out of control and responding selfishly
Just wanting to please self and not really caring about me
I am so sorry darling but you have shown me
A part of you, right now that I didn't care to see

I'm not disappointed and not mad or anything
You just let me know, to stay on bended knees
Pray for your weakness as well as mine
Ask God to strengthen us, because he is always on time
Not only is he on time he also has the power to keep us in line

When we choose to obey. Jesus and only him
He will surely bring us to an expected end

His thoughts for us are good and not evil
He will take care of me, you and every believer
The Devil is a liar and a master deceiver
So I will trust in God as I bend my knees
Cause Sin and Corruption is more than I want to see

MY EXPERIENCE AT THE SPA

My experience at the spa
Reminds me that a lady should be a lady
Where ever you are

I was sitting in the steam room just relaxing
When this man came up and began faxing
Oh well maybe not exactly faxing but conversing
Disrespect, profanity, you name it, and I found it down right embarrassing

I immediately began to feel much disrespect
He was the least bit concern about the things he'd said
This man kept talking until I couldn't hear any more
So finally I just had to kindly let him know

Sir why are you doing all of this cursing to me
I am not one to the fellows you see
He replied so sternly, with no surprise
I have got to do better, because I am a womanizer

He then began to tell me about how he cheated on his wife
Not for a little while but for 14 years of their married life
I actually felt grateful that he had confessed
Because he didn't know that I am an Evangelist

I asked him a few questions that really made him think
Suddenly he stops boasting after I mentioned a few things
Sir do you know that, upon your children you could bring a curse
And the consequences that they may face, could really be worse
I mean really worse than committing adultery with some strange lady

The things they may have to face or suffer; only God can save them

So this man then apologized to me for using all that profanity
I was thankful to God that I could at least say something to help him
More importantly he took the time to just listen
I knew if I had allowed him to go on and on
He probably would have tried to find a way into my heart and home

Why because this man was not a fake or disguiser
He boldly stated I am a womanizer
So instead of this causing me to fear
I had a few things this fellow needed to hear

Oh there is a mirror everyone must face
Just keep living there will come a day
When one must look at your mirror of life either in gratitude or disgrace
You may have to ask the question do I like what I see
Wonder what your mirror reflects could it be peace or misery
Just think about it, you don't have to answer me

No one knows but you what you really feel inside
There are some things going on, that not even you can hide
Sure you can reveal to others only what you want them to see
But deep on the inside, you feel the misery
One thing you realize is; that I cannot hide from me

That's why it is so important for ladies to be ladies
Sin does not care who you are or what your name is
Since I did not allow this man to spread his bad behavior
He ask me to pray for him, when I talk to my savior
He really began to shed tears of remorse and sorrow
He seriously began to think about his children and tomorrow

My experiences at the spa
Really let's me know that it is important
For a ladies to be a lady where ever you are
I truly feel that I have restored someone's family

Otherwise truthfully, the next victim could have very well been me
So ladies before you get involved with, another's husband please
Take the time to stop and think
How would I like it if the wife was me?

NICE MEETING YOU

Just wanted to say it is very nice meeting you
And to also say thank you too
I never really knew what the rice diet was like
No more myths I now have the facts

Thanks to you for the person that you are and all that you do
It is such a pleasure to meet people like you
No joke I am not kidding it is so true
The world would be a better place if we had more clowns like you
Full of laughter, fun, and very serious too

I have no idea where life's journey will end
But it is such a joy to come across friends
As we travel down life's pathway
Looking forward to a brand new day
I hope life bring you much more happiness and joy too
Again I will l say it was very nice meeting you

MR. COMPUTER MAN

I met this friend known as Mr. Computer man
He was always willing to lend a helping hand
He is an expert with computers you please understand
Let me warn you if he can't fix it nobody can

I shared my poetry on Saturday night
While he was checking my home computer out
This man was working and listening too
As I shared my poetry, that was just written fresh and new

I was concerned because I didn't have music
He assured me there was really nothing to it
He said oh yes you will have music tonight
He was very sure, as if to say I know that's right

Just as sure as he stated what exactly would happen
In just a few seconds the music was snapping
I even remember what the music had to say
It was Luther Van dross entitled this is a lovely day

The one thing about Mr. Computer mans style
He likes fixing your computer and seeing people smile
I remember smiling, as he looked in my face
Returned the smile and said see you are having a lovely day

We chuckled a little bit as he prepared to leave
I think he was going to good berries to get ice cream
I really was very happy as he was on his way
Mr. Computer man is awesome what more can I say

So if you are ever having a computer problem

I know Mr. Computer man will gladly help you solve them
And if your computer should ever need a hand
Just call on the help of Mr. Computer man

MR. SPIRITUALITY
HOW DO YOU SPELL MR. SPIRITUALITY?

MANY YEARS AGO
REPENTED OF MY SINS

SAVED BY THE HOLY GHOST

PREPARED FOR GOD'S PLAN

I'VE BEEN PERSECUTED

REJECTED TRIED BY THE FIRE

IN ALL MY TRIALS

TRUSTED IN GOD TO SUPPLY

UNFAILING LOVE AND FAITH

ANNOINTED AND APPOINTED

LIFTED BY HIS LOVE

INSPIRED TO RUN THIS RACE

TODAY AND EVERYDAY

YES I'M FULLY COMMITTED AND I"LL SEE GOD FACE TO FACE

THIS SPELLS MR SPIRITUALITY

I HEAR MY BROTHERS CRYING

Just sitting around listening and chatting one day
I was talking to my brothers and I heard them say
I work hard each and every day
I try to please my wife in each and every way

But while I am trying to be the man
The woman I love don't understand
How much pressure she's putting on me
Cause she is spending so much money I can't even see

I hear my brothers crying I want to take care of home
But the woman I love won't listen and she know she's wrong
She goes out shopping sometimes every other day
And all of the bills I am willing to pay
But she creates new bills and don't want me to say
Nothing about how she is throwing the money away

I hear my brothers crying, while the sister is dying
To get to : not only the shopping mall
But she shops right down the hall
In the bedroom where her computers sat
She gets on the computer and try to buy all she can get

Women we may not like this poetry
But my God someone has to tell the story
When we look around say all men are bad
Some men are the best thing you have ever had

All of the brothers are not incarcerated
Some are functioning the way God created it
They take care of home and they love you too

And you somewhere shopping and acting like a fool
Buying up clothes and brand new shoes
And sometimes that stuff you never even use

I hear my brothers crying she is putting pressure on me
I am not a crack head that's running in the streets
I am home providing just like Gods expects me to be
But her appetite for spending is bigger than she can see
Oh my God my wife and my lover is putting pressure on me
I love her with all of my heart you see
But you bring hardship on the family
Burdens on me financially
I love you honey sincerely
I don't know how I can keep on supplying
The more I try to budget the more you keep on buying
I HEAR MY BROTHERS CRYING

JUST BE CONTENT

Paul says in the holy word to just be content
Not just in some things but in all things in the message he sent
The longer I live the more I began to understand
That everything we experience is already been planned
Not by me, your mama, daddy or any man
Our entire life is guided by the master's hand

So what does that mean to me or you?
I think it would be wise to seek the truth
Haven't you heard that the truth will make you free?
Before we were born Jesus knew all of our needs
We must trust him as we bend our knees
Why because only God knows what's really best for me

Sometimes we chase the wind, going in all sorts of directions
Because we set our own plans and ignore God's blessings
What's even worse is that we will listen to others
Instead of being obedient and listen to God the father
You think I am my own boss so why bother
So we chose to ignore our father who is in heaven
And he is the one who hung bled and died, just to bless us

Unless we learn to do as Paul says, and just be content
We may waste money and time, as our whole life is spent
Making our own plans and chasing the wind
Never fulfilling the purpose of which God intended
And before you know it your precious life has ended
So I am in agreement with Paul, slow down and just be content

THE SUN AND THE SEA

The sun and the sea
Is the definition of a name
What a beautiful name definition
As I sat reminiscing

About the people that has cross my path
Left an impression that's everlasting
As I think about the words exchanged
Thinking about the joys and the pains
As I remember this precious jewels name

Life is like a revolving door
Keeps turning and turning as we go
But as we cross paths with one another
I am convinced that we are all sisters and brothers

We are in this world with all of the same basic needs
We need to give love as well as receive
So as we travel through this life and meet so called strangers
The stranger could very well be your special angel
I embraced that spirit for as long as I could
But God called her home and he better understood
That our time here was up, I tried being all that I could be
A friend, a prayer partner, a listening ear, consistently
But God was now ready to reclaim his son and the sea
I will always remember her; I pray that she remembers me

I DID MY PART

We accomplish so many things in life
Much of the time we have to fight
Fight maybe not physically
But most every time mentally
And most definitely spiritually
Wonder why this has to be

No one ever achieved great success
Without a fight and trying their best
To prepare themselves for the battle at hand
Yes we must fight if we expect to win

I heard a young mother say on her dying bed
As I stood by her bedside watching her take her last breaths
As I stood there helplessly I must confess
My strength was weakening, this was a real test
As I held back rivers of tears at my best
I had done all that I could, I had to rely on God for the rest
So the thing she said that forever lives in my heart
Her final words was; I did my part
This phrase seem short and simple
But yet so powerful as life comes to an end
It is really something to ponder in one's heart
Can we say at the end of life, I did my part?

YOU AIN'T NO FRIEND OF MINE

I wonder where my friend is
The harder I look and the longer I live
I still have not been able to find true friends
Friends will stick with you through thick and thin

One thing I have found out in this world
Is that life can send you in a whirl
You are turning here and turning there
At times and friends can't be found anywhere

I've had people to tell me that they love me
Until a situation came up and they was needed
Perhaps they meant a particular thing you see
I guess anything more, then I'd better look to me

Who knows what that particular thing may be?
Certainly it was not faith and trust and honesty
Just when I needed them most they deserted me
Left me feeling tied up, when I thought I was free

So I began to take life one step at a time
I looked in my own soul, and I realized I was blind
To think that another would always be there for me
Anytime I would really need their help
I come to the realization; I had to rely on myself

But you know our decisions sometimes can prove
That I too, can sometimes play the fool
So I must learn to repent and trust God all of the time
Otherwise I find out even I, sometimes ain't no friend of mine

So others are not always the blame
We have to take a new route, and don't be ashamed
To admit that we are sometimes wrong
Admit we are weak and know that God is strong
Tell yourself that you love you
No matter what others may say or do

So I began to look to God for all of my help
With the natural mind, I couldn't even trust myself
So that's why I call on almighty God for all of my help
My mind has to become more spiritual, I need the mind of God at all times
So I speak to the natural mind, and say, you ain't a friend of mine
I must trust Gods mind at all times

I FEEL YOU

Ever shared your heart with someone
Ever been left feeling all alone
Ever wanted to leave a place call home
Ever wondered why people try to make right wrong
I feel you
Ever tried telling the truth
But the more you told it, the more they lied on you
Ever tried to help some one through
Ever been left feeling used
Ever been left feeling like a fool
I feel you
Ever loved until it hurt
Ever been treated just like dirt
Ever been called a filthy jerk
Ever felt like just giving up
I feel you
Ever felt like you almost there
Only to find out no one cared
Every shedded tears of pain
Ever felt like life's just a game
I feel you
Ever felt if I could blame
Call out every one but my own name
Ever felt sin and shame
But refuse to call on Jesus name
I feel you
Ever felt the wind blow
You couldn't see it but you know
That a breeze is flowing all around you
Folks may lie but the wind is true
I feel this breeze all over me

Ever refuse to believe
I feel you
Jesus knows about all of these feelings
He has all power and he is able and willing
He is just like the wind we may not see him
He is always there if we will just believe it
To take all of our cares, problems, and concerns too
Because he too like me, He feels you

I AM GRATEFUL

There are so many times we take things for granted
We often complain about what we don't have and
Forget about the most precious thing that there is
And that is the fact that God let us live

We may not have everything we want or even need
But at least we have the air to breathe
So for that reason I am glad to be here and be able
To simply say I am grateful

So what has life brought your way?
If nothing else the sun shines today
For eyes to see we should say
I am grateful

So what happened on yesterday?
The stars still shine in the darkest hour
That's by Gods grace and his amazing power
And for that I am grateful

There's no need to even worry about tomorrow
If you can't appreciate today why even bother
To loose sleep and even worry about what it brings
If you are not even grateful for all other things

For legs to walk I am grateful
For a tongue to talk I am grateful
For the love of God I am grateful
God proves to me that he is faithful
And for that I am simply grateful

ONLY ONE STAR

God created this world and the firmaments
Without his creations nothing would exist
Twinkle twinkle little star
How I wonder where you are

Like the three kings of Bethlehem
Following a star and finding a lamb
A lamb born in a stable
A king was born who is able

To make anything he wants you see
He makes every individual what he wants them to be
He says in the book of Jeremiah, it's true
That he knew you before you was formed in your mother's womb

So that let's me know that who ever you are
God is the one, who makes you a star
In every family he chooses one
There is not anything that can be done
To change the fact that you are the chosen one
This choice was made by the Father and the son
For Jesus says that they two are one

Although there are many who tries to put your light out
But the more they try, the more you should shout
Give God praise for his choosing you
And there is nothing that evil doers and haters can do
Don't make apologies about who you are
For it was God, who chose you to become the star

He is capable of making you shine brighter and brighter

He makes you strong, and he is mightier
Than everyone of your enemies
Let your little light shine as you bend your knees
So go ahead and twinkle twinkle little star
And keep shining like the star that you are
Just like the three kings from orient are
In Bethlehem they found only one star

That star is you
Keep shining.

GANG VIOLENCE

Almost daily our young black youth are dying
In the streets of Durham to gang violence
No one seems to have an answer to this problem
So we keep silent and wonder how we must stop this
While mothers are weeping, struggling and crying
Because their babies are steadily dying
In the streets from gun violence

I sometimes ask myself the question why
Did Dr. Martin Luther King even fight for justice and died
Certainly the servant didn't give up his life
For our young brother to become killers of themselves by day and by night
Surely they are blind and cannot even see
How Martin Luther King struggled, suffered and died for equality
For all of mankind especially for you and for me
Martin Luther King died because he stood for peace
Instead of you being thankful, you down with O.G.

Now I don't know a whole lot about the streets
But I have heard a little bit about O.G.
It stands for Original Gangster, who calls himself a leader
One who recruits the vulnerable and began to teach them

I understand they are taught to become expert criminals
They are given weapons, to become cold stone killers
We are not killing strangers, or something or other
My god come on, we killing our very own brothers
Not really truly understanding why
Should I go out and kill, and watch my brothers die
Why should I continue to make mothers cry?
You don't really have an alibi

Don't you want to dry mothers weeping eyes?

Now the police officers decided in and effort to help them
We will set up a place, and pay you for your weapon
Oh my God what a pitiful answer
When guns are being distributed like the spread of cancer
He may sell one gun when he actually owns three
There has got to be a better way to clean up the streets

Now nobody really wanted my opinion or even ask me
But what I think should really happen is for brothers to get down with the real O.G.
That's not for original gangster don't misunderstand me
Listen my brothers you should cop a plea
With our Original God, the one who died to set you free?
And show a little gratitude to Dr. Martin Luther King
If he was living today, wonder what he would think
Wonder would he feel all of his living and dying was in vain
Wonder would he look at what you are doing and feel a shame
Of how you just losing all morals and decide to joined the gang

You may have heard his most famous speech which was I have a dream
I bet he never imagined there is so much killing in the streets
Not by the white man or a foreigner you see
But we are being killed by somebody who looks just like me
Oh my brothers this should not be
When we have not only God, but brothers who died so you could be free

The saddest thing about it is, you can't truly say why
Must you pick up your weapon, and your brother has to die
What we need to do is surrender to deception
Try repenting of our sins, ask God for forgiveness
And try a little more love and affection
Then you can began to be a real true blessing
Try the power of love which is our greatest weapon
And teach others one of life's greatest lessons

Get down with the real O.G. who sets you free
Jesus shedded his blood way back on Calvary
He wants you and me to truly understand
That Love is one of his most powerful and greatest commands

Pride should have no place in your heart
Put down your weapons my brothers and let's try God
It's never to late to make a new start
I'm not trying to be a Savior or anything
I am just simply your sister who happens to love life you see
So why don't you come on my brothers and join me
Come on my brothers, let's get down with the real O.G.

Original God, who created both you and me
Original God who died to set us free
He created us in his image, to Love one another
We were NOT created to kill our brother
He commands us to love as he has loved us,
He is not begging it is a must
You see Jesus Christ is the Man
And one thing you must clearly understand
That his Love is not optional it is a command

Please don't hate me because I tell you the truth
I just simply say and do what God tells me too
From my heart I say to you: My brothers, Love You Peace,
on behalf of Dr. Martin Luther King
And all those other men who fought for justice, peace and equality
my friend
You are not in Iraq or Afghanistan
If you are down with the real O.G. then let's make a change
And do it in Jesus Name
Last but not least, My brothers: I never had to run from a Klu Klux Klan
I shouldn't have to run from a black man

HAPPY BIRTHDAY TIWANA

There is no birthday like your birthday
It is kind of like burger king you get to have it your way
But don't get to overly excited, let me say
This is only for your birthday
That you get to have it your way

So may God bless you today to do as you please
While I take a pause and go down on my knees
There is no telling what my little eyes may see
As you get to do as you pretty well please
I wish you God speed and many more of these

These days of joy fun and laughter
Happiness today and forever after
As you are surrounded by friends on your special day
It is my prayer that this kind of joy will remain always
This is your special day, so do what you like
Let the joy of the lord, continue to abide
As he grants you love and peace and be your guide

May the love of God guide you to fulfill your purpose
As you live life to the fullest and overcome every hurdle
Let your spirit leap and jump for joy as you trust God and pray
Let the joy of the lord be your strength from day to day
May you and God, have it your way
May you live love and laugh as you lift your voice
I wish you much peace, from my heart to yours
Well there is so much more that I could say
But it probably would take a couple of days
Don't want to bore you, so anyway
I love you girl, May God Bless you and Happy birthday

HAPPY FORTY FIFTH BIRTHDAY

Lord have mercy you are forty five
But I love you dear brother of mine
Hope God bless you with many more birthdays
And hope he blesses you in miraculous ways

He has already blessed you very much I know
I have seen how God has allowed you to grow
Into a man who have learned to value life
You are a man who avoids trouble and strife
You love your God your family and your wife
I thank God for your sacrifices

You turned away from a destructive life
And decided to let darkness go and walk in the light
I know your buddy says you are a half century old
But I am here to tell you brother I know you are a blessed soul
A heap sees but a mighty few knows
What road you may have traveled, but Gods in control

Your mother gave birth but God gave the gift
The gift of life, so that you might live
Not just today or tomorrow you see
God wants you to live abundantly
So for that reasons he supplies more than enough
I am wishing you a happy birthday and I love you my brother

Now I only have one last thing to say
I will still whoop you in trouble on your birthday
I want you to have fun, laugh and play
But I will still spank you in trouble on this day
Nope when it comes to trouble you can't have it your way

GOD BLESS YOU MY BROTHER AND HAPPY FORTY FIFTH BIRTHDAY

Love your Big Sister
Phyllis

HAPPY BIRTHDAY SISTER

I couldn't think of a better card
Than one written from my heart
There are so many wonderful things to say
I will just begin with, Happy Birthday

I pray that this day you will find
Unspeakable joy that is so divine
So as you began to go on your way
May your hearts desire be granted this special day

I thank God for allowing me to meet you
May he richly bless you, in all that you do
I'm happy to have you as a friend of mine
Just like Jesus it is so divine

I have given it some thought, but never understood
The real true meaning of sisterhood
So on today I can truly say
I love you and happy birthday
Thank God for sending you my way

A woman with such loving and unselfish ways
May God bless you on your birthday and everyday
I would give you the world today if I could
To show my appreciation for your sisterhood

Now may God open up heavens doors
Shower down on you blessings and much more
Than you and I could ever know
Enjoy your birthday as you live, learn and grow
As heaven smiles upon you with such a glow

May the rays from heaven continue to shine
And May God keep blessing this dear friend of mine
I will always remember you when I pray
There is not much more I have to say
Except God Bless You and Happy Birthday

HAPPY BIRTHDAY BUSTER

Well Buster I searched high and then I searched low
I couldn't find a card in nobody's store
That would be appropriate for your day you know
So I decided to my computer I would go

I am wishing you a happy and bless day
When someone is as smooth as you it's hard to find words to say
So since that is such a difficult task
I will simply try to do my best

I wish you many more happy birthdays
I pray that Gods blessings shower you day by day
It is such a blessing how you and all your friends
Allow everyone else you know to come and share and join in

To celebrate your special day
I thank God for allowing me to come your way
It is such a loving spirit in what you guys do and say
May God richly bless you with many many more birthdays
Well I tried my best that is all I could do
May you continue to be too smoove

MERRY CHRISTMAS ANGIE

Well Well Well what do I say to and Angel
You are almost as precious as that little baby in the manger
Maybe I shouldn't put you up quite that high
But honestly Angie in my book if you had wings you could fly

Soar with the Angels as they travel to and from heaven
Angie in my life you have truly been a great blessing
There was some days when my mind was quite tensed
The words you would say to me would help me relax

So as I told Michael it was hard to find a card
To say what I want to say coming straight from my heart
Life can take us in a spin and some pretty difficult places
Your professionalism and kindness to me was like a soothing eraser

The words that you would always say
Would help calm my fears and bring peace my way
Isn't that just like Christmas even in July
When I think of your kindness tears of Joy I cry
For you have been like an Angel standing by my side
In my heart you will always be flying high

The gift that we all truly needs
Cannot be found under a Christmas tree
It is too big to be wrapped in a box
Cause the most precious gift is found in the heart
Love is in my heart for you Angie
God Bless you and Merry Christmas to you from me

THIS GOLDEN CANDLE

Well Merry Merry Christmas Friend
And a happy new year too
I couldn't find the right card
So I made one especially for you

I remember you searching for a big big candle
Finding a big big candle seemed a little hard to handle
I was hoping you would find the big candle from the start
But since you couldn't find a big one
Here is the biggest one from my heart

This candle may not be as big as what you were looking for
But to me it so much bigger because it means so much more
It's not just another little candle or another card
This is a little golden candle straight from my heart

The more gold is burned the better it shines
That is exactly how our life goes sometimes
So with this golden candle
And golden trimmings too
I want you to always remember
There is a friend who's praying for you

What I want you to do when things come to make you
Sad or blue
Just look at the golden candle
And remember a friend is praying for you

I pray this Christmas will find you full of laughter and joy
As the days go by after Christmas you will find more and more
Things that make you happy in this coming New Year

May God bless you friend
Maybe you will catch a rein dear
Oops rein deer

I know that makes you happy

ETERNAL BREAD PUDDING

Thank you Jesus for White Flour for it represents the Purity and Holiness of God

Praise Your Name for the Sweet Milk for it the sincere milk of Gods Word for all the babes in Christ

I give you Glory for the Butter it represents Sins being resolved into repentance

What a Blessing to have Sugar it is for the Sweet Holy Spirit of God

Thank you Jesus for the Vanilla Flavor it enhances the taste: Oh Taste and See that the Lord is good

I Magnify your name for the (3) Eggs for it represents the
TRINITY,
Can't have one without the other FATHER, SON, and HOLY GHOST

Bless Your Name for the Yokes of the egg representing he Spirit of Bondage being broken by the Power of God

I have Got to Praise him for the Raisins, which represents the Fruits of the Spirit
Meekness, Temperance, Love, Joy, Longsuffering Galatians 5

Hallelujah anyhow for the 3 spoons of Cooking Oil that represents the Anointing of God, which is that Yoke Destroying Burden Removing Power,

This takes care of all the lumps and bumps of life, it make rough places smooth, it make hard lumps become soft, it makes the difference in how things turn out it your life.

The Anointing Makes the Difference it gives you power to live a life so God can get the Glory as you prepare to meet him for your eternal home in heaven

Jesus is the true bread who has come into the world for our sake. We need the Bread of Life to sustain us in our lives.

This is just a little cake I was commanded to bake by the Holy Spirit Hope you enjoy it. Oh taste and see that the lord is good

FAREWELL

Life is something to be cherished
God created man in his own image
He didn't expect the body to stay
So he sent his son Jesus to prepare the way

He came hear to earth in the form of a man
Then he died and left his spirit so we all could stand
He made a way so that we could be free
Yes Jesus made a way for both you and me

He knew that we would need a resting place
This earth down here is just a temporary space
He promised to never leave us nor forsake
God is supreme and he makes no mistakes

No this place is not our home
Although we may get lonely, but we are never alone
Jesus went away to prepare an eternal home
I realize we must depart this life to reach that throne

Although I have known you for many many years
I may think of you and in your absence and shed a few tears
But when I think of how you took hold of Gods Child
The tears will soon turn into a smile

Because I know that you have to be in a better place
For your spirit must be rejoicing, on this very day
I believe in my heart, you would say don't worry for all is well
Because you made the choice to hold on to Jesus unchanging hand
So Jesus reached down to pluck his flower
Because he knew the time the place and the hour

Although you have been in the family for many years
Jesus knew when he would draw you nearer
So Jesus hears our every cry
He will never ever pass you by

Darling you will be truly truly missed
I know that God knows what is best
He decides when it's time to take a rest
God has spoke and we must accept
So I simply say, sleep on, sleep on and Farewell

THANK YOU

Life is such a precious gift
No matter how short or long anyone may live
God is the giver of all good and perfect gifts
He gives us life and the power to fulfill

Not one but everyone of our dreams
Without God it is impossible to do anything
Even a little simple thank you which may seem small
If God didn't wake me up, I couldn't even call
On him or anyone else
So first I must thank God for all of his help
Second I thank God for my great grand daddy's life you see
Because without God and him there would be no me
So I thank God for his life he gave
I thank GOD for the family he made
I thank grand daddy for the family he raised
and last but not least I thank God for his amazing grace
My thoughts and memories are filled with joy and happiness
I love you grandpa but I know god loves you best
THANK YOU

WHEN SHACK STARTS BURNING

When the shack starts burning
And there is no water around
Throw the kids out of the window
And let the shack burn down

This little piece of poetry use to make me laugh
My grandma told it, I thought it was the best
Little piece of poetry I had ever heard
I remembered every little word

I didn't realize until I was grown
That granny really left a legacy of poems
Many of them I cannot remember
But it occurred to me that her poetry had entered

Deep into my spirit and so now I write
She never wrote poetry a day in her life
But I realize she had so much to offer
She is now deceased but all is not lost because

I must write and tell my stories
But the real truth is granny was a great poet
She died and left this world and no one even noticed
That a real legacy is gone on, with granny called poetry

I know she is up there in heaven above
Gloryifying the king and the heavenly dove
She was filled with so much history and love
So what she may have dropped, I will now pick up

I must keep writing and tell the story
Grandma you keep praising, God and I'll write poetry

In memory of Harriet Wiley
(Love you Grandma)

UN COLOR ME

I live to be free
But
Am I free to live
In a society that colors me
Color me, color me don't you see

It is my color that won't let me be free
No one will admit but I do know
My color, My color is half the story
Half of the reason why I can't really be free
Cause I live in a society that colors me

Life should be painted LOVE, this is my belief
My question is how can this be , can you tell me
If everyone could be color blind
And just uncolor me, please uncolor me
Maybe then I'd stand a half of chance to just simply be free

Many may wish to be good and wealthy
Some may cry just let me be healthy
Life has its many valleys and peaks
All I want is: Please uncolor me
I just want to be Free Free Free

Race with me, Rise with me or maybe Disagree
This may not be your flavor or your cup of tea
But I say Only real LOVE will let me be free
Will you just let real LOVE uncolor me

Color has carried too much weight
It is color that paints the gruesome word hate

Let's not allow color to determine our fate
Uncolor Me, Uncolor Me and let us recreate

Uncolor Me Black, uncolor me White
Let LOVE be the color for everyone's life
Rainbows never had a problem
Colors blending and beautiful as can be
If we behaved like rainbows
Maybe just maybe we could all be free

Rainbows blend without a problem
If we thought like rainbows we could solve them
Old bitter, pains, of color bruises and battles but
Instead we are like sheep that all have been scattered

We could have a much better blend
If only you would uncolor me my friend
Uncolor me that 'tis all I need
Then maybe in this society, I can truly be free

Uncolor me and just see my heart
This is the only way to make a new start
Breaking down walls of separation then we could
Build love and freedom with great anticipation

Uncolor me and Let me be free
I will love you being you, will you let me be me
Uncolor me and Set me free
I only see Love, Tell me what do you see

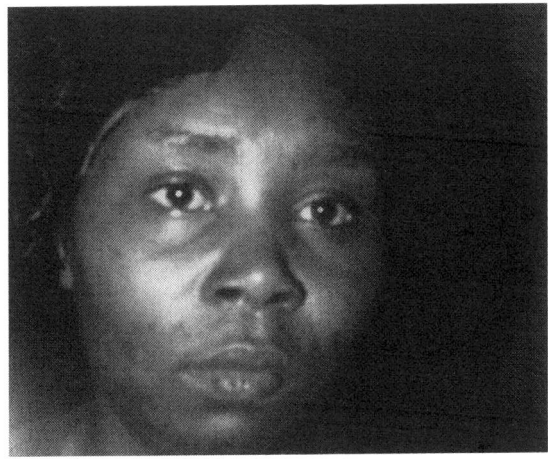

(one of my deepest pains)

THE MOST DANGEROUS STRANGER

The thought came to my mind one day
Of just how precious life is, and how loving is a little baby
I don't think there is a greater time on earth
Than a mother going through pain and giving birth

Born into this world are men and women
Enemies and also friends
There was even a baby born in a manger
As a matter of fact some may even call him a stranger
His name was Jesus and he is a true friend
As a matter of fact he gave up his life to free us from our sins

And everyday is born some friends, enemies, lovers, and even strangers
But the most appauling thing that strikes me as dangerous
Is when you have to look a love one in the eye
The one whom you rocked all night when they cried
Or maybe you stuck right by their side
When every one else would run and hide
Making up excuses and alibis
Ducking and dodging and telling lies

    Sometimes some of the most ungrateful people
Are the ones who always had someone there whenever they needed them
    It is really a sad day when we have sisters and brothers
Incarcerated for years because they killed their own mother

    I try to be calm but I sometimes become angered
When I realize too many family members have become strangers
Forgetting about that little baby who was born in a manger
Instead of loving one another we become the most dangerous stranger
I know we wish to ignore the fact that this is true
My only concern is, which one are you?

Jeruselem **OBITUARIES** 33 AD

Calvary

Jesus Christ, 33, of Nazareth,
died Friday on Mount Calvary, also
known as Golgotha, the place of the skull.
Betrayed by the apostle Judas,
Jesus was crucified by the Romans,
by order of the Ruler Pontius Pilate.
The causes of death were crucifixion,
extreme exhaustion, severe torture,
and loss of blood.

Jesus Christ, a descendant of Abraham,
was a member of the house of David.
He was the Son of the late Joseph,
a carpenter of Nazareth, and Mary,
His devoted Mother. Jesus was born
in a stable in the city of Bethlehem, Judea.
He is survived by His mother Mary, His
faithful Apostles, numerous disciples,
and many other followers.

Jesus was self educated and spent
most of his adult life working as
a Teacher. Jesus also occasionally
worked as a Medical Doctor and
it is reported that he healed many patients.
Up until the time of His death,
Jesus was teaching and sharing the Good News,

soulgraspingpoetry.com

ISBN 141209751-7

Edwards Brothers Malloy
Oxnard, CA USA
May 20, 2014